POTTING PLACES

D1441715

POTTING PLACES

Teri Dunn

FRIEDMAN/FAIRFAX
PUBLISHERS

For Mary Jowell, with love

A FRIEDMAN/FAIRFAX BOOK

First paperback edition 2001
©1999 by Michael Friedman Publishing
Group, Inc.

Library of Congress Cataloging-in-Publication
Data available upon request.

ISBN 1-58663-249-3

Editor: Susan Lauzau
Art Director: Jeff Batzli
Designer: Lori Thorn
Photography Editor: Wendy Missan
Production Manager: Camille Lee

Color separations by Colourscan Overseas Co.
Pte. Ltd.
Printed in China by Leefung-Asco Printers Ltd.

1 3 5 7 9 10 8 6 4 2

Distributed by Sterling Publishing
Company, Inc.
387 Park Avenue South
New York, NY 10016
Distributed in Canada by Sterling Publishing
Canadian Manda Group
One Atlantic Avenue, Suite 105
Toronto, Ontario, Canada M6K 3E7
Distributed in Australia by
Capricorn Link (Australia) Pty, Ltd.
P.O. Box 704, Windsor,
NSW 2756 Australia

Please visit our website:
www.metrobooks.com

Contents

A PLACE TO POT

*I only went out for
a walk and finally concluded
to stay out till sundown,
for going out, I found, was
really going in.*

—JOHN MUIR, FROM *THE LIFE AND LETTERS OF JOHN MUIR*, PUBLISHED IN 1923

You have just returned from the garden center with several flats of your favorite annuals and a big bag of potting mix. You stow them on the front porch, open up the garage, and root around until you find last year's window box inserts. Oh dear, you didn't clean them out very well—old soil is crusted on the sides, and they're covered in spiderwebs. Time for a trip to the hose! You might as well do this right and make sure there are no lingering soil diseases, so you go into the house to fetch a scrubber sponge and a jug of bleach. Oops, you forgot gloves, so you head back indoors again. Finally after much scrubbing, the window boxes are clean and ready for the new season.

Now it's time to pot. You spread out on the patio or lawn, within reach of the hose. You know that pouring the soil straight into the window boxes isn't the best way to begin, so

If you enjoy gardening, you owe it to your plants—and yourself—to organize your supplies and tools and set up an agreeable workspace. A potting place brings a whole new dimension of pleasure to gardening.

once again you go back inside and get the largest mixing bowl you can find in the kitchen. Now you're ready.

A tedious hour later—after awkwardly scooping out handfuls of mix from a corner torn in the sagging bag and filling and refilling the bowl, then dampening the mix, squeezing it out, and pressing it into the window boxes—you're tired, hot, covered in dirt, and only just beginning to tuck the plants into their spots. When you finally finish, you creak to your feet, your back stiff. You haul the filled boxes into their usual spots out front, maneuver them into place, and step back. This is the moment when the gardener should feel pride and joy. But, honestly, the whole process felt just like a chore.

And you still have to clean up. So you roll up the bag of unused potting mix and stick it in the garage; make a decision about saving or discarding the flats the plants came in (you could sow those blue-flowered columbine seeds in them); hose off the spot where you were working; wash out the bowl; and then wash your hands. Whew.

Or, how about this scene? You've started a bunch of your favorite herbs from seed. Soon they are up and outgrowing their flats, and it's time to move them

Above: Potting up a favorite houseplant, such as this amaryllis, becomes a fun job when you can work on a comfortable, ample surface, use the right tools, and choose from an assembled array of containers. Opposite: You may become so fond of your potting shed that you leave the door propped open all day as you come and go, working on various projects.

into pots. You pick a time when the family is not hovering around and mealtime is not imminent, clear off the kitchen table, and cover it with newspapers. You carry over the flats. You fetch some small plastic pots, which are hopefully clean and ready to go, and some potting mix.

First you prepare the pots. Again this means moistening the soil mix first, in a large mixing bowl. Getting into an assembly-line frame of mind, you moisten the mix, squeeze a handful, press it into a pot, take a chopstick or pencil and make a hole, then push the pot aside. After a dozen, or two, the table is crowded. Maybe, to your annoyance, one or two tumble off the table and have to be retrieved and refilled (you can clean the floor later).

Now for the transplanting. Should you sit down or stand up? Both options are awkward. You end up hunching over the table, a fork in hand, gingerly lifting out tiny seedling after tiny seedling, gently transferring each one into its new home. If the day grows dark, you turn on an overhead light, but your own shadow dims your view of this tedious work. When you're finally finished, your eyesight is blurry and your back aches—and the kids are trooping into the room demanding dinner.

Been there, done that? Well, maybe it's time to consider a place to pot. If you have a good spot for one or are willing to make room, why not construct, or invest in, a true potting shed? It can be as plain or elaborate as your needs and resources allow. And imagine—you could do all kinds of projects under its roof, rain or shine, in comfort, with the convenience of every tool and supply you might need readily at hand.

If a structure sounds too ambitious or costly, certainly it is time to consider purchasing a potting bench or portable caddy or setting up a modest potting "corner." No matter what you decide, you want a place designed and appointed by you, a place that will make so many gardening chores easier.

Gardeners who realize they have "crossed the line" from casual weekend gardening to true devotion to (or obsession with!) a beloved hobby all eventually come to this point: they straighten their aching backs, eye the mess they've just made, wonder why all their tools and supplies are always in disarray, and say, "It is time." The defining moment is probably similar to the feelings of cooks or bakers when they, too, critically eye their inadequate kitchen design and supplies.

If you are such a gardener, this book is for you. If you are ready to be more efficient, neater, and faster at your cherished hobby, you need a place to pot—and to do many other gardening projects, from cleaning pots to making cuttings to transplanting rootbound houseplants to dividing bulbs.

Part of the fun of setting up a potting place is decorating it—the space shouldn't be purely functional any more than a garden

Gardeners, no less than the plants they tend, relish natural light, so a table set up by a bright window is an ideal situation. While working, you can enjoy the same contemplative pleasure you feel when you wash freshly picked produce or dishes at the kitchen sink while glancing outside.

is purely functional. Inside a potting shed you can indulge in bundles of dried flowers and herbs or you can hang up a few botanical prints. Outside, you can paint the trim or the entire structure in jaunty colors or in hues that harmonize with your garden. A potting bench or area also allows plenty of opportunities for creativity, like employing unusual or "found" materials such as tiles, a vintage washtub, or supports made from bent wood. Anything you do to individualize your potting place doesn't just make the spot your own—it makes you look forward to working there.

Don't forget that a potting place not only cheers and motivates you, but it benefits your garden as well. Because you are working more efficiently, you tend to think up more projects and execute them more successfully. Neatness and productivity at the bench translate to healthy new plants out in the garden and inspired ideas for their placement. When you have a potting place, your garden gains a fresh new sense of purpose—and pleasure.

The following chapters will guide you through the many options available, in terms of design and layout as well as tools and supplies. If you need still further persuasion, numerous sidebars highlight projects that are easily accomplished in these potting places.

In the end, the greatest benefit of all—no matter how modest or how elaborate your potting place turns out to be—is that it is your domain, dedicated to your love of plants and gardening. When you swing open the door of your potting shed or deliver flats of just-arrived plants to your potting table, you'll breathe deep the rich and fertile aromas of soil and growing things. Then, to echo John Muir's sentiment, you'll discover that going out to your spot is "going in," entering into an absorbed and contented state of mind that is the gift of a good working environment. You'll enjoy the anticipation of heading "in" and, when you finish, feel a resounding sense of satisfaction.

Truly, this is a new world for your plants and a place to nurture your garden in a great variety of ways. And it is also a new world for you. It is a dream come true. As every gardener knows, dreams nourish the soul as well as the garden.

Above: High sides or backsplashes are always a smart feature of potting tables. Opposite: Once in place, a potting area can become an extension of the garden itself; plant vines to adorn its sides, set potted flowers out front, and let other plants encroach on their own.

Chapter One

The Essentials of Potting Spaces

As with planning a well-designed and well-appointed kitchen, giving careful thought to a potting space's working conditions is your first step. Attend to siting, access, light, and storage before you begin the fun and individualizing steps of loading in supplies and tools. This chapter will help you with your decisions, offer thoughts on the advantages (or disadvantages) of various features, and provide tips to make things more efficient.

The "macro" issues ought to be thought through and attended to at the outset. The goal is to set up everything right the first time, so you don't have to make a move or major alterations later.

Siting and Access

There are probably many places around your home or yard where you could set up. Your main concerns are putting your potting place out of the way of traffic (careening kids, the car, the path of the lawn mower) and in a location that is convenient not only to the garden but also to running water and perhaps electricity. And, obviously, you want a relatively level spot so the building or table won't wobble and water from rain or the hose won't pool under it.

If you choose to keep your potting spot indoors, such as in the basement or garage, you need to make sure to keep it out of the path of household traffic. You don't want children or pets rooting through stored soil bags, fertilizers, or garden chemicals or knocking over pots.

For an indoor water source, a spot adjacent to the laundry area might work. You won't want to clog the utility sink, but you can plan to fill watering cans at its faucet. Alternatively, look into installing a faucet in your potting spot. It's a minor job for a plumber, especially when there are nearby pipes to branch off from, so it shouldn't cost you an arm and a leg.

Above: Ideal conditions for such projects as potting up seedlings include not only good light but also plenty of elbow room and nearby water. Right: Organize your potting place so that heavier items (big pots, bags of amendments) have support and smaller or fragile ones are not in the path of any traffic. Here, large items are stashed behind a pretty counter skirt.

GIVE IT SHELTER

Shelter is also important to consider. Woe to the gardener who absentmindedly places a shed or table outdoors under or next to a drainpipe, leaky gutter, or eaves that shed rain onto the area. Protection from midsummer's blazing hot sun—for your comfort as well as that of the small plants you may be working with—is equally desirable, so avoid placing your potting spot in an exposed location. Shelter and shade can easily be provided by an ample overhang, a large tree, an existing (or newly installed) awning, laths or a pergola (with widely or narrowly spaced wooden slats), or even a beach umbrella, perhaps on a deck or patio.

One big advantage to a potting table or caddy is that it can be fairly portable. Outdoors, you can experiment with it to find the best location, or you can simply work in different spots depending on the time of day, the season, the weather, or your whim.

A TRUE RETREAT

Since a potting shed is obviously going to be a good-size addition, it needs to be sited with special care. A gardener who prefers seclusion may tuck a shed into a back corner of the yard. This way, the shed does not overwhelm or shade the existing garden. This approach has the added virtue of allowing you to make a path to the shed's door

Above: A potting table is your opportunity to consolidate and organize all the tools and pots you have accumulated. Left: It's wise to set up a worktable in a sheltered spot—overhead protection from rain and the hot sun will be appreciated by you as well as the plants, tools, and supplies.

(perhaps, if your yard allows, a winding one, just to make the approach more private and fun). Otherwise, someplace off the garage or behind the house may work well. Bear in mind that nearby or accessible amenities, such as water and electrical outlets, will make outfitting the shed easier.

Creating a potting corner or setting aside a spot for a potting table can be trickier—the territory may need to be shared and is therefore tougher to protect. Ideally, your potting area should not have to compete with other household items, such as a grill, trash receptacles, or laundry bins. If it does, it's doomed to play second fiddle, be pushed aside, or be treated thoughtlessly by the nongardeners in your household. If you must protect its sanctity from others, cover it when it is not in use with a large tarp or blanket, or erect screens or other barriers around it.

A STAGING AREA

One last consideration: it's helpful if your potting area can act as, or is adjacent to, a staging area. Flats of seedlings that need attention, such as thinning or watering, can wait there until you bring them to your tabletop. Overgrown houseplants that you want to remember to divide and repot can be stashed in a staging area until you're ready. Freshly purchased supplies can be brought there from the car, and later be taken in one by one and stowed in their

Opposite: A potting shed tucked into a secluded corner of the yard becomes a true retreat; just remember to consider how you will get the amenities of water and electricity back there, should you decide you want them. Right: A "staging" spot just outside your shed or adjacent to your table can store work you are planning to do or display recently completed jobs.

appointed places or used to replenish bins that are low.

A good staging area is a spot you are in the habit of keeping clear until needed. For a potting shed, it might be a flat area, flagstone, bench, or small table outside the door (but not in the way of hurrying feet or a swinging door). For a potting table, the staging area might be just a few square feet on the ground to the right or left. To designate a staging area, border it with stones, bricks, or wood or lay down a mat or some salvaged wooden pallets—anything that marks the spot for the purpose.

Light

"A clean, well-lighted place" is the phrase made famous by Ernest Hemingway. He was talking about a place to write, of course, but gardeners certainly have their basic needs,

Above: Potted plants outside a shed door greet the gardener and visitors alike with their cheery, healthy appearance. Place them out of range of the swinging door and spaced far enough away so that equipment (wheelbarrow, mower, etc.) doesn't bump them coming and going. Opposite: While potting tables are fine places to repot and harden off various plants, they are no substitute for a greenhouse and often end up being too cool and dim to allow the plants to thrive. Thus, plants tend to be visitors rather than residents.

too. Whether you are sowing tiny seeds or sharpening a hoe, your safest, best, and most enjoyable work will be done in a spot where you can see exactly what you are doing.

NATURAL LIGHT

A dark spot doesn't just feel like a cave, it suffers from the same liabilities—namely, difficulty seeing your hands and your work and finding what you need, not to mention poor air circulation and dampness. A source of natural light is always ideal, especially for a gardener, simply because a sense of the nearby outdoors is a balm and an enticement. Windows or a skylight that you can crack open is best. If too much light floods in, you can always mount a shade or curtains to give you the option of moderating or blocking it. And early in the morning or late in the day, beams of sunlight will be welcoming as well as illuminating. Plus, during the heat of summer, windows give you the chance to let in some cooling fresh air.

For indoor potting tables or corners, a spot under a window is nice, assuming that the backsplash and shelving areas don't block the light. This way, you can enjoy the same contemplative pleasure you may feel when you wash freshly picked produce or dishes at the kitchen sink while glancing out the window.

If you decide to locate your potting place outdoors, don't set it on the south side of the house or garage in full sun. You will bake in the hot sun, as will the plants or seedlings you are working with at the time. An eastern or western exposure is better.

Setting your potting bench in front of a bank of windows assures that you'll have an abundance of natural light. Make sure, though, that you have a supplemental light source for those inevitable cloudy days.

ARTIFICIAL LIGHT

Artificial light is essential for working at the beginning or end of the day, or on dark or rainy days. Plus, you may prefer to have light you can always count on or light you can direct, which can only be supplied by a lamp or lamps. Or you may have set up shop in a spot that has little or no natural light, such as the garage or basement.

There are many options available to you, assuming your spot has access to electrical outlets. Overhead light is nice because shadows are less of a problem or are eliminated, but don't overlook the possibilities of portable or flexible lamps. There are some ingenious ones that can be mounted or clipped to a shelf or benchside. (Grow lights, intended for raising seedlings, are not appropriate.)

One final note: just as in the house, both traditional lightbulbs and fluorescent ones eventually burn out. Be sure to store some extras in a place where they won't get knocked, kicked, or toppled. This way, you won't have to pause for long when a light burns out.

LIGHTING SAFETY TIPS

Always use caution when working with electricity. Here are a few guidelines to ensure safety:
....

• Don't do your own wiring. Hire a licensed electrician, even if the job looks easy. A professional knows all the safety precautions and whether a circuit can bear extra power points or a new one should be wired.

• Keep in mind that water and electricity should not mix; site their sources, as well as their paths, safely out of range of one another.

• Consider having a GFCI (ground fault current interrupter) at the outlet. This inexpensive and highly valuable feature automatically shuts down the electricity in the event of an overload or surge, and resets after the problem passes.

The Work Surface

Attend to the surface on which you will work, and you will never regret it. The whole point of having a potting area is to make life easier for you. You have a number of options; choose according to your needs, budget, and taste.

A good work surface can be anything from a salvaged table of some kind to a potting "bench," a structure built expressly to make potting work comfortable and convenient. Gardeners before you have discovered that the best surface is one that slopes slightly downhill toward you, for easier cleanups and to prevent water from pooling. It's also nice, though not absolutely mandatory, to have edges mounted on at least the back of the table (a "back-splash"), if not also on the left and right sides. This helps prevent soil mix from cascading off in the heat of a project—plus the edges can stop a pot from going overboard.

The potting surface itself ought to be fairly smooth. When potting benches are fashioned from rough wood, dirt tends to accumulate quickly and becomes difficult to remove or scrub off, particularly if the joints are not tight. (Slats are downright impractical, difficult to work on, and difficult to clean.) Plus, you might get splinters as you work or tidy up. Smooth wood surfaces, on the other hand, work very well.

Charming as they may be to look at, decorative surfaces—such as old tin ceiling tiles—may present cleaning difficulties. Ceramic tiles need to be well-grouted into place and, if possible, the grouting should be level with the tiles themselves to facilitate cleaning. A metal surface, smooth or ridged (such as is sometimes used with household sinks), is not hard to clean, though rusting can occur over time.

Storage

If you are ready to devote an area or entire outbuilding to potting and other garden projects, you are already convinced that you want to consolidate your supplies in that spot. Your options are many and depend on not only how much stuff you plan to cram in, but also how efficient you want to be and how creative you care to get with receptacles.

Above: Small or less-used supplies can be stowed on upper shelves. Left: Potting benches come with a variety of practical, valuable features. Raised sides and a raised back keep both supplies and pots from going overboard.

You can't have too many shelves, cubbies, and storage bins in a potting shed—after all, this is your chance to really get organized and to make access convenient. It's fun to also allow room for some decorations—such as pictures and vases of fresh flowers—among the practical items.

SHELVES

Upper shelves are the simplest means of keeping what you need handy. Traditionally, an upper shelf is not very broad, though it runs the length of the potting table for maximum efficiency. It should have a raised edge or rim along the back so nothing falls off. An upper shelf is mounted above and behind your work area, so it doesn't interfere with your mobility. With many potting tables, it is simply attached above the backsplash area.

Needless to say, a smaller shelf is not meant to hold heavy items. Use this valuable spot for tools you use all the time, such as your trowel, a dibble, or a small watering can. Or put on it supplies you use regularly, like plant tags, small boxes or bottles of plant food, and so on. Alternatively, you might line up or stack small pots here, so they'll be handy when you need them.

Some gardeners mount hooks or small holding caddies, or incorporate molded tool slots, along the upper shelf. These additions make good spots to hang gloves or favorite implements.

Lower or adjacent shelving is extremely useful, and provided the shelves are sturdy

enough (strong wood or other material, well-supported and well-anchored) and broad enough, you can stow bags, boxes, baskets, and tubs on them.

Shelves can be mounted above, below, or adjacent to your workspace. But keep height in mind! Potting soil and other amendments, especially when stored in quantity, are heavy. Plan to store them lower to the ground or floor, even on the lower shelf under the potting surface. This way you can just reach in, rather than having to pull them off each time you need to get at them.

CUPBOARDS

Any storage area with a door looks neat and is safe (assuming you can lock or latch it). Here you can place sharp tools or garden chemicals that should be kept out of reach of children. And the door can be turned into extra storage; just mount a little hook or nail and hang your gardening gloves or apron on it.

Note that if you mount a cupboard outside, it should be watertight and have a rain-shedding, sloping roof.

CONTAINERS

Bins, tubs, and boxes are so helpful you will quickly wonder why you didn't invest in them long ago. Every gardener knows the minor annoyance of flopping-over bags of potting mix, and the way, after it gets low, you always have to reach way down into the bag just to scoop out what you need. If you've come this far, make life easier for yourself. Get some large

Cupboards are wise acquisitions because you may wish to stash little-used or potentially dangerous items (garden chemicals or very sharp tools, for instance) within. This keeps them away from small children and pets, and it also reduces clutter in your potting area.

containers and keep the supply bags in the wings for refills. This is the gardening equivalent of flour and sugar canisters in the kitchen.

DRAWERS

As any handyman can tell you, drawers right below your work surface are a godsend. You can access the tool or supply (string, tape?) you need quickly and close the drawer again to keep the other items in it safe, clean, and out of reach of little hands. (Of course, occasionally you will have to haul out the whole thing and clean it.)

If you have the space, consider bringing in an old dresser (summer yard sales are a good source). Most have about four drawers, and the drawers are wide and deep enough to store almost any hand tool, bags of bulbs, and other medium-size residents of the potting area. Or fill entire drawers with potting soil and amendments (except, probably, fine sand), and label each one. If the drawers are not snugly constructed or have warped a bit with age, you may get some spillage, but generally it's minimal.

Drawers just below a work surface are extremely handy. Store your favorite or most frequently used tools here and you can complete any task without missing a beat. Other drawers, as in a file cabinet or old bureau, may also turn out to be very useful.

Water

An ordinary potting surface becomes downright efficient and convenient to use when you include a sink, allow for drainage, or both. Because the height of a potting table is already comfortable for you to work at, the sink can either be set on the tabletop or sunk into the surface. The whole idea behind having a sink is to work neatly and avoid wasting unused soil or amendments.

CATCHALL SINKS AND TUBS

The most primitive tables have a hole cut in the top and a receptacle of some type positioned below. The simplest option is just to set the source bag or bucket right below, saving you a transferring step later. Otherwise, use a tub or bucket. A box is fine if you are planning to sweep only dry materials into it, not water. No matter what you use, don't forget that it should be broader than the hole or drain above it, so it does its job of catching everything that falls.

Catchall receptacles allow you to work quickly and efficiently, scooping away excess water or soil. You can attend to cleaning it and reclaiming the leavings later. A simple screen mounted across or under the hole can be a good idea, for it directs the unused material and filters out big chunks or pebbles—so you're sifting even as you work, which is a nice plus.

MOUNTED SINKS

A sink or bowl set right into the table is another way to go. It's closer to your work, of course, plus the mess is confinable. Waste lands in the sink or can be scooped into it. Deeper sinks hold more refuse, and you don't have to keep interrupting your work to clean up.

If the sink is removable, cleanup becomes a cinch: you just haul it out and dispose of or re-store whatever has gathered in it. Weight can become an issue at this point—a very

While some gardeners manage a potting place without a sink, if you are able to install one, be assured that it will be in constant use, as so many gardening projects seem to require water. You have many options, from full plumbing with hot and cold taps and a drain to a simple, removable plastic basin; there are many variations between these two extremes.

CLEANING SUPPLIES

Here are some items to keep handy for post-project cleanups:

....

- Regular household sponges
- Scrubber sponges
- Scrubbing brushes
- Steel wool
- A dull butter knife
- A sharp pocketknife
- Rubber gloves or a box of disposable surgical gloves (no need to get sterile ones)
- Liquid soap or bar soap

- Bleach
- Solvent (for rubbing off sticky tape or glue), such as nail-polish remover
- Cloths or old rags
- Q-tips
- A nail scrubber
- An old toothbrush
- Moist wipes (restaurant "moist towelettes" or diaper wipes)
- A hand broom or brush
- A dustpan
- Hand lotion

Perhaps the easiest, least expensive, and most portable option for water in a potting place is the good old watering can. Keep it constantly filled so you don't have to trot over to the faucet in the heat of a project or when you notice that a plant is thirsty.

deep sink full of sodden soil or sand is awkward to yank out and carry, and you may find yourself bailing it out at some point. Also, the material the sink is made out of determines its weight: a full ceramic sink is pretty unwieldy, whereas a full plastic one is easier to maneuver.

If you prefer to have a permanent mounted sink, just be sure that it's seated securely and, if appropriate for the material and your table's surface, well-grouted or sealed into place.

DRAINAGE

A hole that lets out water and other liquids only (fitted with a removable strainer or very fine screen to facilitate cleaning) is very nice to have. Naturally, you have to give some thought to where the waste is going. A bucket stationed below is safe, easy, and cheap. It should hold more volume than the sink so you can use it for a while before having to empty it (of course, a big bucket or garbage can full of water or sodden soil can certainly be a challenge to empty).

Alternatively, you can install, or hook up to, actual plumbing. If you're already planning to have a plumber come out to install a faucet, consider going all the way and having drainage attended to as well. It will have to run into your household waste water system, whether town sewer or septic tank. Pipe size might become an issue, so you should talk it over with the plumber and emphasize that some particles, not just water, plus the occasional garden chemical, will be flushing through.

NO DRAIN?

As with most situations in life, there are pluses and minuses to installing a drain in your potting area:

....

Pro:
You can fill a tub or bowl with soil, soil mixes, and other amendments with impunity, free of the worry of washing clogging clumps down a drainpipe or constantly clearing a strainer.

Con:
You are probably going to have to empty and clean a drain often, if not after each use. Not impossible, but you may come to see this chore as a hassle after a while.

Resourceful gardeners can scare up many of the furnishings they need for their potting places in junk shops, flea markets, and yard sales. Here, an old laundry sink has been installed into a potting bench. Its worn surface makes it durable enough for constant and sometimes rough use, plus it lends an air of vintage charm to the setting.

WATER SOURCE: GETTING AND DELIVERING

The serious gardener wants to have water handy to wash hands, pots, and other containers and clean off soiled tools. And, of course, handy water allows you to pre-dampen potting soil, water seedlings and plants, and moisten cuttings. Getting water into your potting place can be as simple or elaborate as you like, or can afford.

The easiest way to have water on hand is just to stock the spot with one or more watering cans (see sidebar on page 36). Fill them at your nearest water source before you get started, so you don't have to interrupt the momentum of your current project. And, assuming you'll be back soon, make a habit of refilling them before you depart, so they'll be waiting and ready for your next visit.

FAUCETS, HOSES, AND WATERING GADGETS

The next simplest way to have accessible water is to have a faucet nearby. It can even be your hose faucet or one just like it mounted next to your worktable. If you have the choice, set a convenient height for your faucet—either a few inches higher than your deepest watering can or perhaps at hip or arm level next to your table. A swiveling feature might be worth looking into, so you can swing it into position as needed and move it out of the way when finished.

When you prefer to water or wash something in your garden using a watering can, the weight is sometimes a bit much. Save yourself the strain and take cans with you in a wheelbarrow or wagon if need be.

To extend a faucet's reach, use a long or short hose, or invest in one of the many attachments available from garden supply catalogs and well-stocked garden centers. An on/off trigger is essential because you don't want to be running back and forth to the faucet or drenching your workspace. Watering wands are especially nice because you can alter the fineness of the spray as needed, from soft and diffuse for misting tiny, tender seedlings to full-on pouring for filling or rinsing the watering cans or buckets. At specialty greenhouse suppliers you can find especially nifty prod-

ucts, including coiled cords that have a long and flexible reach when you need them to, but take up little space when not in use.

If you decide to invest in plumbing, make a decision about how elaborate you want to go (see the information offered earlier on sinks and drainage). And don't do it yourself; hire a professional plumber. Because plumbers charge an hourly rate, maximize the productivity of their visit by having the chosen site ready and all the pieces on hand (sink, drain, faucet, washers, even pipes if you know what is needed).

RUNNING HOT AND COLD

Having both hot and cold taps is a luxury, no doubt about it. But access to hot water can really come in handy some days. Steamy water always seems to benefit a good scrub given to stubborn, crusty dirt or residue. You'll also be able to fill a watering can or spray tender plants with the tepid (rather than icy) water they prefer. Last but not least, after long hours working in chilly ground or in an unheated area, it sure is nice to lather up your dirty hands with warm, soothing water.

A watering wand allows you to deliver the fine spray that little seedlings and young plants prefer. Check specialty garden suppliers for a variety of useful gadgets like this.

Owners of potting sheds and tables often joke that watering cans, like clay pots, seem to multiply when they're not looking. It's true that you can be seduced easily by the myriad practical and charming choices available, and come to favor different cans for different uses...until, one day, you find your collection has burgeoned. As long as you have the storage space, why not continue to collect these essential tools? One advantage of watering cans that we often forget is that you can control the water temperature within them. Hose water is often quite cold and therefore unwelcome for vulnerable little seedlings starting out life in a cold frame or being hardened off on the porch. Tropical bulbs and houseplants also appreciate less-than-freezing water.

Plastic vs. Metal

Traditionally, watering cans have been made of galvanized steel, zinc, or copper. The metals are very durable, and such cans may last for years, especially if they are well made with reinforced seams and so forth. Copper is a very soft metal that is easily dented, but it is a sentimental favorite, especially because it ages to an appealing aqua-tinged patina.

Plastic cans, however, have many merits. They are much lighter, which is a benefit when you are carrying them full of water or hefting them high to deliver water to a window box or hanging basket. Their smooth handles don't dig into your hand like the handles (or, more egregiously, the swinging wire bail that some hardware-store models have) of metal cans, especially when full. Because plastic is eminently moldable, you'll notice a much greater range of designs and sizes in the plastic watering cans.

In recent years, cleverly made plastic cans that look like metal ones have appeared on the market. They might be worth considering—you get the best of both worlds, the attractive look you want in a lightweight tool.

A Rose Is a Rose?

A good watering can has a removable rose (the "sprinkler" at the end of the spout), which can be taken off for cleaning when it becomes clogged. The option also allows you to use the can when you don't need or want water to spray, such as when you are moistening a bowl of potting mix or topping off a pebble-filled tray at the base of a humidity-loving potted houseplant.

The best roses are made of brass because this metal takes a fine punch well, leading to a better, more uniform spray. Brass also corrodes more slowly than plain metal, so a brass rose lasts longer. Other roses will do a decent job, but won't last as long.

A well-made watering can is a joy to use and fun to display. A little hunting around in specialty gardening catalogs, gift shops, hardware stores, estate sales, and flea markets will allow you to quickly amass a diverse collection.

You should get extra roses at the time you purchase your watering can, since roses can wear out or get damaged and replacement roses always seem so hard to find when you really need them.

Cleaning Tips

Scrubbing your watering cans is not an especially wise thing to do—unless of course they become completely filthy and unusable. Abrasive sponges and cleaners can actually damage and wear down the surface of metal cans (especially copper ones), and scratch the surface of plastic ones. It's better just to rinse out your cans with a little bit of water as needed or wipe them down occasionally with a damp cloth.

The one part you should clean is the rose, which may become clogged with debris. Flush it out at the sink or with a stiff spray from the hose. Or swish it in a bucket of soapy water. Obviously, this is easier to accomplish if the rose is removable.

Note: Watering cans should not be used for delivering garden chemicals of any kind—diluted or otherwise, particularly toxic ones—to plants. There is the danger that you will forget and unintentionally deliver a fungicide or pesticide to an unsuspecting plant via lingering residue in the can (plastic cans, especially, can harbor such residues). Or someone else, unaware of what was in the can last, will do the same thing while helping water your beloved plants.

Storage Ideas

First of all, try to keep your cans out of the sun, which causes the paint-coated and plastic ones to age prematurely. Fortunately, this is no problem for owners of potting sheds and potting tables.

Here are a few ideas for handy places to keep your watering cans:

• Jumble them under the potting table on the lower shelf, safely out of the way but within easy reach.

Hang your watering can collection aloft to add character to your potting place and to keep the cans out of the way until you need them. Just be sure the hooks are strong and that they are high enough so that you don't bang your head!

• Stack a few, one atop another, with the bigger ones on the bottom.

• Mount hooks for them on a wall or ceiling (if it's high enough) and hang them by their handles. Employ hooks that extend far enough and are strong enough for the job.

• Mount a rope or a bungee cord overhead or in a window in lieu of a curtain rod, unhook one end, string on a few watering cans by their handles, and reattach the end. (This is only practical with smaller cans; big ones are too heavy and bulky.)

• Hang them by their handles from an old-fashioned coatrack.

• Line empty ones along a high shelf, not just to keep them out of the way, but also to display their decorative appeal—they'll look like a jaunty little parade.

Essential Tools

Every gardener has his or her own needs and prejudices regarding tools, but there are a few basic tools that are common to all potting places. Since they will be heavily used, it behooves you to buy quality tools that won't need replacing soon and are a pleasure to work with.

Trowels: It is probably a good idea to have more than one of these indispensable tools. You'll use them for scooping and moving loose materials from soil mix to pebbles; filling flats; digging out seedlings, bulbs, or rootbound plants; and no doubt performing other activities as well. Some come with measuring marks (inches or centimeters or both) down their fronts, eliminating planting-depth uncertainties.

Pruners: The best ones are precision tools, comfortable to heft and a joy to cut with. There are many models and sizes to choose from, so take your time and pick one that suits you. If you're left-handed, by all means get the model designed for you. If you have small hands or arthritis, give your hands a break with a set that has lightweight fiberglass handles. "Rachet" pruners use an anvil action that requires less squeezing (however,

Above: If your gardening supplies and implements have been scattered in various places, or if you've held off acquiring certain items, consider the establishment of your potting place a golden opportunity. Be creative in displaying and storing them—try caddies and baskets, as well as the more obvious options of hooks, drawers, and shelves. **Opposite:** Having the right tool for the job—and a place to keep it—is one of the joys of potting places.

they don't allow a flush cut). If you're a bonsai enthusiast or like to do close-in, detail trimming, little bonsai pruners (which resemble modified scissors) are needed.

Cutting tools: Always keep a pair of scissors and a sharp pocketknife around. Both are handy for opening seed packets and bags of soil, amendments, and other horticultural supplies. If you are an aspiring propagator, a grafting knife is a good thing to have in your tool collection.

Writing tools: You'll want a pen or pencil to make notes to yourself in a gardening notebook, on a seed packet, or in the margins of a catalog or reference book. Indelible markers are good for plant labels or even for scrawling on the side of pots or flats.

Seedling helpers: Every gardener, it seems, has a favorite implement for making little holes to set seeds in and for later removing small plants to larger quarters. Traditional bulb dibbles are just too bulky; a pencil or straw might do the trick in some cases. Regular forks, cocktail forks, spoons large and small, popsicle sticks, chopsticks, and knitting needles are all possibilities.

Tools for outdoor use: Assuming you have the space, your potting area can also house implements such as shovels, cultivators, forks, hoes, rakes, shears, loppers, hedge trimmers, saws—perhaps even a ladder.

TAKE GOOD CARE OF YOUR TOOLS

For cutting tools of all kinds, always keep the cutting surfaces sharp and clean. Sap and pitch easily gum them up; if dirt ends up adhering to these surfaces, you've got a sticky mess. Needless to say, a dirty or obstructed cutting surface means more stress on your hand and wrist, as well as sloppy cuts.

Moisture is the enemy of most tools, corroding and rusting them in short order. Make a habit of wiping and drying off trowels, pruners, knives, and so forth after each use. If you don't plan to use a tool again soon, or are storing it for the winter, a light coating of oil wil protect it from rust.

NICE BUT NOT ESSENTIAL

Here are some useful items you might enjoy having in your potting place. You can live without them, but they can make certain gardening projects easier or help you with maintenance.
....
- Chalkboard or bulletin board (for displaying notes, reminders, and lists)
- Apron
- Magnifying glass or hand lens
- Clothespins
- Stapler
- Tape (scotch or masking)
- Plastic wrap
- Small plastic bags
- Bulb dibble
- Hammer
- Screwdriver
- Large scoops or cans for scooping
- Measuring cup
- Flower-harvesting snips
- Flower press
- Spray bottles
- Kneeling pads
- Paper towels
- Tarp or blanket

TOOL CARE SUPPLIES

Keep the following items on hand, and you'll always be prepared to care for your tools properly:
....
- Old rags
- Small can of lubricating oil
- Sharpening files
- Steel wool

Opposite: An orderly system of hooks isn't just tidy, it helps you keep track of what tools you have and lets you survey your choices easily. Right: Tools with prongs or sharp tips are best stored so that they don't poke you.

TOOL STORAGE

Where you store your tools—on a wall, hanging from a shelf or benchside, or in some sort of tub, bin, or drawer—is up to you. No matter what you decide, however, there are some basic principles.

• Each tool should have a place. Remember, your decision to have a potting place stemmed partly from the wish to be more organized, so avoid chaos and inefficiency, and assign everything a spot. You can always change spots for a tool that you find you are using more often than you thought you would.

• Keep like tools together. This may mean bundling all the pens and pencils with a rubber band or stuffing them into an accessible pot; putting all the trowels in the same drawer or bin; or keeping all knives together so you can view your choices when contemplating a project that requires cutting.

• Protect sharp edges. Sheathe your pruners in a holster, if they come with one, or wrap them in a cloth. Store knives that fold in the folded position; store those that don't fold safely out of reach of small hands.

If space permits, store larger gardening tools and equipment in your potting place. If you're still in the planning stages, you'd be wise to write in enough space for this purpose. It's wonderfully convenient to have everything in one place finally.

SUPPLIES FOR OUTSIDE USE

In addition to the supplies you'll need for potting, your shed or potting corner can also store the necessities for tending the garden:
....
• Tying and fastening supplies: twine, including the nylon kind; string; twist-ties; rubber bands; and clips.

• Stakes: bamboo, metal, bulb support, Y-stakes for floppy perennials, and so on. Since they are too tall to be proped up in an unused pot, store them in a big vase, bucket, or clay drainage pipe, upended.

• Garden plastics: row covers, black plastic, and hardware cloth.

• Cloches, hotcaps, and other season-extender gadgets, such as Wall-o-Waters.

• Wire: chicken wire, screen, etc.

• Racks: various sizes of purchased or home-made wooden racks, so useful for drying certain vegetables and herbs.

• Sprayers, nozzles, hoses: either for watering or applying garden chemicals.

• Winter plant-protection aids: burlap, wood, plastic, wire, stakes, and so on.

Basic Supplies

Here's your chance at last—the moment you've been dreaming of—to gather together every material you use or want to use on a regular basis. With a potting place, at last you can buy in bulk (storing the excess if necessary) and reach what you need when you need it. What a thought!

Your first shopping spree will be the most expensive, of course, no doubt partly fueled by your excitement about stocking up at last. Over time, it will become clear to you which items are truly staples. You may also modify your storage system as you settle in. Some things you might pick up include:

- Potting soil
- A seedling-starting soil (sterile potting mix)
- Perlite and vermiculite
- Dehydrated manure
- Sand (coarse builder's sand, not beach sand)
- Pumice
- Lime, gypsum
- Fertilizers
- Liquid, powdered, and tablet plant foods
- A soil test kit
- Rooting powder
- Garden chemicals (weed killers/herbicides, fungicides, and pesticides)

No longer do you have to toss pots and containers into unruly piles in the garage. By storing your containers in an orderly manner, you'll have a clearer idea of your inventory. If you can, get into the habit of cleaning them before you need them, so that they'll be ready at a moment's notice.

POTBOUND

You may elect to buy a selection of various pots, both clay and plastic, just so you have them on hand and can grab what you need when you need it. (Don't forget drainage saucers.) But, as you will quickly discover, pots accumulate. So don't go wild at the outset.

Clean your pots: If you recycle pots (and what gardener doesn't?), it's smart to clean them before you pile them up. Make up a solution of nine parts water to one part bleach, dunk them, wipe them down, and rinse them off. Intensive scrubbing is generally unnecessary—the bleach will kill off any lingering pests or diseases even if their residue is not completely removed from the inside of the pot.

Broken clay pots: Your precipitously leaning stack of pots falls over and many of the pots break. This is not a tragedy, it's an opportunity. Scoop up and save the small pieces and chips. They're great as filler and drainage in the bottom of deep pots or planters, or those that lack drainage holes.

Plastic seedling pots: While you may reuse some of these to start new seedlings, the smallest ones, which come in pods/flats from every garden center (each pot only about two inches [5cm] across), really accumulate. You know who needs them? The garden centers you got them from; they are often willing to take back the pots for reuse in their greenhouse operations.

The Comforts of Home

Every potting place can benefit from these extras, which over time may begin to feel like essentials to you. These can include a:

• Fan, to provide relief on hot or humid days or to dissipate fumes.

• Refrigerator, within which you can store bulbs, stratifying seeds, and cold drinks. You might pick up an old one at a yard sale or buy one of those little "dorm fridges."

• Chair or stool; even when your potting bench is at a comfortable height, sometimes you want to "take a load off" or sit down to write notes. A true chair, such as a rocking chair or an old easy chair, is your reward when it's time to take a break—or when you want to offer a visitor a comfortable vantage.

• Hook, for a towel, jacket, sweater, raincoat, or your straw hat

• Boot scraper or mud tray, so you don't track in dirt or mud from the garden

• Trash can; it needn't be very large; most gardeners are great recyclers and don't throw out much.

• Coffeepot or radio; if you have electricity at hand, why not indulge yourself with a few amenities?

Left: A potting shed certainly should have features that make it comfortable and attractive as well as practical. Ample floor space, plenty of windows for natural light and ventilation, and attractive nearby landscaping are all features that make it enjoyable. Above: Nice extras include a small refrigerator. Use it to pre-chill bulbs, stratify seeds, and store a few cold drinks for yourself.

Chapter Two

Potting Sheds

The great moment has arrived. You've decided to put in a true potting shed, a place to call your own. The amount of money you want to spend may be a constraint, but think of this as you would any other building project—while the structure may cost more than you initially wanted, you don't have to do everything at once. This chapter will guide you through the choices you must make and the options that are available to you.

Siting

Even if you have a spot in mind already, walk around your yard and see if there are other possibilities. Ideally, you want to erect the potting shed in an area where it will not interfere with the garden already in place or other uses of your yard. You may be dreaming of an out-of-the-way retreat, but don't forget that if you want accessible water or electricity, the most remote corner may not be the best idea. Also, local codes may not allow you to put a shed too close to a property line or publicly owned area.

Some gardeners romanticize the image of a shade tree right next to their humble hut, casting dappled shade and sheltering songbirds to enjoy as they work. But such a location is not always wise—large roots under the shed make for a wobbly foundation, and removing them is generally neither practical nor good for the tree.

A little site preparation is in order, unless you're installing the shed on ground that is already unused and bare. Rope off the area and dig out whatever is growing there. Sod can be delivered to the compost pile; perennials in decent condition can be divided and given new homes elsewhere in the yard. Dig out and move large stones. Rake the area smooth.

Then, if you think it's necessary, lay down a layer of small gravel, which can help avert any drainage problems (if you anticipate more than the most minor, post-rainfall

The best location for a potting shed is one that provides easy access to your garden but doesn't allow the structure to steal the spotlight. A path and thoughtful landscaping help it fit into its surroundings.

Drying Herbs

A favorite activity of herb gardeners is drying herbs for future use in delicious dishes, seasoned oils and vinegars, sweet-smelling potpourris, and craft projects.

Materials you will need:
sharp scissors or snips, paper towels,
a wooden drying screen or rack
(not metal, which may react with
herb oils). Optional materials:
brown paper bags, string.

The key to success is careful harvesting. Make your move in mid- to late summer, just as the herbs are starting to bloom. It is then that the volatile oils, which account for the wonderful scents and flavors, are at their highest levels. Pick in midmorning, after the dew has dried. If the herbs are dusty or dirty, gently wash them and blot them dry.

Good air circulation will ensure quality dried herbs. Lay leaves and sprigs on a screen or rack, not touching one another, in a hot, dry place out of direct sunlight. A shelf or other undisturbed corner in your potting shed may be ideal.

Alternatively, bundle twiggy herbs and hang them upside down, again in a warm, dry place. If there's too much light or you're afraid the drying leaves will fall off and disperse, put a paper bag over the bundle, and cut slits for ventilation.

A potting shed allows you to see a project such as drying herbs through from start to finish—you can sort, bundle, hang, and display your handiwork on the premises.

puddles, it would be smart to elevate the shed above ground level). This layer will also keep out opportunistic weeds (until the shed itself shades them out or smothers them). Last but not least, the gravel will provide a flat surface for the structure to perch upon.

Despite your best efforts, the site may not be totally flat. There are a number of ways around this: you can prop up one end or side with bricks or cinder blocks (in problem spots or in soft soil such as sand, install concrete "piers"), or shore up gaps with loose stones, bricks, or slate shims. If worse comes to worst, or if you just want the security, you can pour a concrete foundation.

Remember to be a good neighbor. If your shed will be near a property line, be sure to mention your plans to those neighbors. If the structure in some way offends them, it is better to sort this out in advance.

Here is a shed that, though small, offers many benefits. It is open enough to have good light and air circulation, it has a sloping roof to shed snow and rain, and it is neatly organized inside.

Dimensions

Some potting sheds are cozy little outbuildings, no bigger than a child's playhouse, while others are ample enough to hold all the things you want them to plus bulky equipment, such as the lawn mower, chipper-shredder, wheelbarrow, and so forth. No matter what your plans are, the same caveat for planning a new garden bed applies here: you'd be wise to make it bigger than you think you want at the outset. You won't have any trouble filling it up, and later expansion may be impractical or impossible.

You don't need to be an architect to design a nice little shed. Consult books that offer plans (see Further Reading) and modify them if you want. Also, before you decide anything, it's a good idea to visit other gardeners' sheds and look them over carefully; even bring a measuring tape if you wish. Sketch out on paper what you have in mind and make a shopping list of supplies. Of course, if you don't have a lot of confidence in your carpentry abilities, you should get help or hire someone who is more experienced.

Make sure to build enough height into your potting shed: there's no point in setting up a cramped space. Much of your work will be done on your feet, at the potting table, and you don't want to be banging your head or

Above: Make your shed roomy enough to easily accommodate all of your potting things—you don't want it so crowded that you can't work comfortably.

Opposite: Plan your potting place's layout around the largest item, namely the worktable or potting bench.

A well-designed potting shed will be in scale with its surroundings. A sloping roof sheds rain, while the large window takes advantage of a southern exposure, a slatted cupola provides ventilation, and wide doors accommodate even the bulkiest deliveries.

hunching over. This is why co-opting a child's playhouse may not work—you're just too tall! Bear in mind, too, that if you'd like to install shelving or hang watering cans, certain tools, or dried bouquets from the ceiling, you'd better allow for ample headroom.

While many of our homes may have eight-foot (2.4m) ceilings, with an attic or crawl space above, the same design in the shed is not necessary. Consider leaving the interior rafters exposed and open. Unless you live in a fairly dry climate or want to do a lot of sealing and caulking, don't chance a flat roof. A sloped or peaked one is best, covered with roofing material or shingles that shed rain and snow and keep the interior dry.

Don't go too high. A twelve-foot (3.7m) -tall shed may look out of proportion. To help you decide on length and width, take into account the dimensions of the shed's largest residents. The potting bench will be a focal point and probably your biggest item: let's give it an ample six to eight feet (1.8 to 2.4m) of space lengthwise, with several feet on each side of it to stow supplies or tools. Other big pieces to allow for include storage cupboards (maybe three or four feet [91cm to 1.2m] long) and cabinets (up to six feet [1.8m] long). Will you have a stool, a chair, a file cabinet, or barrels and bins?

SHOULD YOU BUY A POTTING SHED?

Just as with homes (think of the log cabin kits), you can purchase a prefabricated potting shed or commission someone to make one for you. If it comes assembled, it will have to be hoisted (by strong arms and backs or a crane) into position. The delivery and setup can add considerably to the cost, so be sure you know what the total is before you agree.

Aware that there is a growing trend in America for potting sheds these days, some enterprising garden supply houses are offering kits. Some are partially assembled; others are nothing more than a pile of lumber and hardware. If you're not up to assembly, hire someone competent; if you are, you still may need some help. It goes without saying that the instructions should be read very carefully before proceeding. Mail-order sources of potting shed kits are listed in the appendix. Be forewarned that you can spend anywhere from $1,000 to $4,000 on a pre-fabricated potting shed. One way to save money is to buy a plan or blueprints only; buy the materials you'll need locally.

Increasingly, potting sheds are available in kit form, which may be the way for you to go if you aren't an accomplished carpenter or amateur architect. Generally, they're well-designed, and all the pieces you need—from boards and shingles to hardware and windowpanes—are provided.

Make Your Own Potting Mix

Plants that begin or spend their lives in containers need a good medium to grow in, not the heavy, possibly weed-laden soil of the yard. Of course, you can buy potting soil, but many gardeners discover that it is sometimes too light or has the wrong pH for certain plants and that some doctoring is necessary. Note that all of the following ingredients are available at any garden center; feel free to modify the recipe.

Materials you will need: peat moss, sterile loam, and sharp sand or perlite. Optional: ground limestone, a pinch of bonemeal.

Scoop equal amounts of the peat moss, loam, and sand or perlite into a tub or bucket, and mix everything. Remember to moisten and squeeze out the peat moss and loam first, or they won't absorb water well once in the mix.

Modifications: If you are potting succulents, add more sand or perlite to improve the drainage. If you are potting acid-loving houseplants, such as African violets, increase the amount of peat moss. If you are potting an alkaline-soil-lover, such as a cactus, add a bit of lime. A small amount of powdered bonemeal is believed to give potted plants an extra boost of nutrition.

One of the joys of having a potting shed to work in is doing things the way you've always wanted to—including making your own customized potting mixes.

What about the door—will it whack something every time it swings open?

Finally, after your shed has been stocked with furniture, tools, and supplies, will you have room to move around without banging your shins or elbows? The point here is that now is not the time to be conservative—estimate your needs generously. Naturally, you are free to customize, but a modest potting shed with some or all of the above items generally ought to be twelve feet (3.7m) to fourteen feet (4.3m) square. A smaller one may do, but it can begin to feel cramped. If you have no choice but to keep it small, then scale back your plans for its furnishings accordingly.

Of course, nobody says a potting shed must be a perfect square. If you prefer a rectangle or an L-shape, plan to place the potting bench or table against one of the longer sides and place the door in the opposite wall. Other shapes, such as the octagon so popular in gazebo designs, usually turn out to be impractical for a potting shed because you do need a long wall or two, for the potting bench at least.

DO YOU NEED A BUILDING PERMIT?

Check with your local planning department before you start. If the structure you have in mind is more than 120 square feet (11m²), some areas—especially densely populated urban and suburban areas—require you to take any variety of the following steps: submit your plans for approval, obtain a special permit, apply for an easement, and/or pay a fee.

If you hire someone to erect the structure for you, make sure the two of you discuss this issue, and see to it that the builder attends to the necessary paperwork on your behalf. This isn't merely red tape; part of the idea is to ensure that people build structures that are safe.

The Next Round of Decisions

After you decide on the size of your shed, you need to plan for a number of essential and practical items that will make your daily use of it agreeable. If you aren't comfortable being the architect, visit other gardeners' sheds and study the plans in instruction books for ideas (see Further Reading).

CONSTRUCTION MATERIALS

Metal is for those awful, stifling, spiderweb-strewn storage sheds your father always stowed the lawn mower and hose in. And, unless you are modifying a brick or stone structure, the effort and expense of using these materials for a new shed is often prohibitive. (Also, brick and stone buildings are nice and cool in summer but absolutely freezing in winter.) So it is most likely you will make your potting shed out of wood. It is the best material for the job, and it makes customizing easier, whether you design your own or alter someone else's plans.

Another advantage of a wooden shed is that it can be insulated, which, if you live in a cool climate, will make it possible for you to use the structure on chilly mornings or evenings as well as during the winter months. The insulation can be fastened between studs and rafters before the interior walls are covered with plywood or drywall.

Simply contructed of wooden planks, this potting shed is remarkably practical. While small enough to comfortably occupy a typical backyard, it is yet roomy enough to hold the essentials of a gardener's craft.

Above: If you're a pot collector, be sure to designate a shelf or corner of the shed for display or storage. Left: All sorts of materials, including salvaged ones, can be employed in the construction of a potting shed. Wood or wood-dominated ones are generally the most comfortable, durable, and inexpensive.

Not all woods are created equal. As you might expect, quality and durability cost more—you have to pay for longevity. Remember that in addition to the exterior being exposed to the elements, the inside of your potting shed is going to see its share of dampness, both from the water you use in your various projects and from mud you or your visitors tramp in. No matter what wood you choose, you should treat it with a coat of water sealer. Staining or painting the outside adds further protection.

The following are some traditional materials for potting sheds:

• **Redwood:** Popular as a deck material, it is indeed pricey, but is beautiful and naturally rot-resistant.

• **Pressure-treated lumber:** Much more affordable, this wood is usually pine that has been treated with chemicals that prevent it from rotting when it comes into contact with moisture, soil, and fungi. (Garden author Roger B. Swain aptly calls it "embalmed wood.") This means you can count on it to be long-lived. However, it's not terribly attractive, so staining or painting it may appeal to you. Ask at the lumberyard about products that are known to adhere well to the surface of pressure-treated wood.

• **Pine:** It is inexpensive, and if you are not looking to spend a lot of money, why not? It looks great initially, but soon weathers to gray; damp weather causes it to warp and eventually rot. You can arrest this process by coating it with a wood preservative, not just at the outset, but on an annual basis.

• **Rot-resistant, seasoned woods:** These include cypress, cedar, poplar, locust, and others. If these are available locally in the sizes you want, and you can afford them, they're good alternatives. Cedar siding is a nice material. Cypress is especially long-lasting, thanks to its native habitat of swamps.

• **Plywood:** This material is very cheap and prone to warping. If you decide to use some on your shed, be sure to purchase plywood

intended for exterior use, and don't expect it to last a long time.

• **Scrap wood:** Many an enterprising gardener has made a shed, or part of a shed, out of scavenged wood. Pieces of an old barn, construction-site or demolition castoffs, even old shutters—almost any wood can be pressed into service by a creative carpenter. The longevity and weather protection such materials provide may not be the best, but you may enjoy the results so much, you are willing to compromise in other areas.

THE FLOOR

You have several options for your floor, and your decision will be dictated by the nature of the site you've chosen as well as your personal preference. If the spot doesn't have drainage problems, and you don't mind the shed being a bit primitive, you can certainly just leave the floor as bare dirt or lay down an inch or two of pea gravel. If you've poured a concrete foundation, you may be satisfied to just let that serve as the floor. Another option is to lay some boards (treated wood or redwood, please!) on

the ground. To make the surface more substantial, you could add bricks, pea gravel, or more lumber atop or below that layer, or both.

WINDOWS

The difference between a potting shed and a storage shed is that the former is a pleasant place to linger. Light makes all the difference. Your potting shed should have at least one window, if not more. You will enjoy the natural light and fresh air it lets in, and the whole place will feel more homelike. You

Left: Screens in potting shed windows are not mandatory—you may find the cross-breezes quite pleasant, plus you'll feel closer to the garden. Of course, when winter comes, you'll have to take steps to protect whatever you decide to leave inside. Accents such as a container of long-blooming annuals, as above, contribute much to a shed's appeal.

may decide to forgo a screen in the window, as long as you don't mind an occasional fly or moth winging its way through—unlike your house, the potting shed is a more rustic, close-to-nature place.

A nice plus to having a window or two is that you can hang curtains, blinds, or a shade. Or you may wish to put a stained glass ornament or light-refracting crystal in it. Alternatively, line bottles, jars, or pots on the window sill and fill them with small plants or cuttings or leave them empty to provide simple decoration. Outside, you can add shutters (either decorative, or the kind that close) and mount a window box underneath. Again, these are welcome, homey finishing touches that are completely up to your discretion.

If you happen to live in a neighborhood where someone might be tempted to break into your shed, the ability to cover or seal a window when you're not there, so no one can peer in, also doubles as a security measure. (A lock on the door is then also advisable.)

EXTRA LIGHT AND VENTILATION

If your shed is small, or if you want lots of light, consider adding a skylight. If it can be propped open on hot days, so much the better. Or you might include an operating cupola, mounted on the peak of the roof. Design it with slatted sides, but a protected roof, and you'll get extra ventilation plus additional, though diffuse, light.

THE DOOR

Should the door swing out, or in? In is preferable. When you hang things on hooks on the back of a door, which you probably will—your raincoat, straw hat, or even a favorite rake—you probably won't want them exposed to the elements. Better to have the door swing in, where the wall it meets (or a doorstop) will effectively make it act like a closet when opened wide. The only disadvantage to a swinging-in door is that you may sometimes forget what's hung on its back or stashed behind it.

Some people have fun tracking down and installing a vintage door of some kind, perhaps from an old house or farm structure. Bear in mind that the severity of your weather can shorten the life of an inexpensive door (especially a salvaged one originally intended for indoor use). And no matter what you choose, a door that seals tightly when closed is wisest. This keeps out not only spitting rain and drafts, but also off-hours visitors like the neighbor's cat or a curious skunk. For balmy summer days, or days when a gentle, warm rain is falling, you may wish to prop open the door; or you may want to install a screen door. A door with a top half that can be swung open separately is another option. Don't forget an interior latch, a hook-and-eye latch, or a lock if you think that's necessary.

The principal advantage of an inward-swinging shed door is that the back of it can double as a storage spot. Attach hooks for hanging tools, a jacket, or hat, and tuck shovels, rakes, and other tall or unwieldy implements safely out of the way behind it.

NOVEL DOORKNOBS AND HANDLES

While most good home-supply stores have all sorts of choices of knobs and handles, there are more ways to have a little fun with your potting shed door. The following are a few whimsical ideas that other gardeners have employed:

....

- Drawer pull
- Trowel or weeding fork (you'll have to solder on some attachment hardware)
- Vintage bathtub faucet handle (hot or cold!)
- Oven handle from an old-fashioned stove (some are porcelain beauties)

A finishing decorative touch, such as a vintage or artistic doorknob, adds immensely to the charm of a shed.

Latches and locks on doors and windows are advisable if your shed is in an area where intruders (neighborhood kids, cats, or even curious raccoons) might tamper with the contents when you're not around.

PLUMBING

Water is not a luxury in a good potting shed—it's a necessity. Unless you plan to run out to the hose spigot or into the house to constantly refill watering cans, you are going to want running water piped in. Your simplest option is a basic faucet. For true luxury, you might decide to put in a hot-water tap in addition to a cold one.

If you also want your potting shed water piped out (that is, you want a sink that drains into the sewer system pipes or septic system), the idea becomes more ambitious and, naturally, more expensive. But think of the convenience and seriously consider making the investment. Be aware, however, that this is generally not work you can do yourself. Building-department codes require that plumbing for any residential structure be done by a licensed professional. And there are often regulations about what sorts of pipes you may install. However, in the case of running out a simple faucet, or sink that drains, you may be allowed to save some money by using plastic or PVC pipe rather than the more costly household copper piping.

While you may be perfectly used to running back and forth to fill a watering can, indoor plumbing will likely be the smartest investment you make in your new potting shed. You'll quickly come to consider running water an absolute necessity, not a luxury.

Mount a simple faucet in your shed, one that is no more elaborate than a hose spigot, and you will find that you use it constantly.

Softwood Cuttings

If you enjoy taking cuttings from woody plants or have resolved to try this technique now that you at last have a proper work space, a good place to get started is with softwood cuttings. These are easily taken and prepared in late spring or early summer.

Materials you will need: a sharp pair of pruners; a jar of water; rooting powder; pots; vermiculite, perlite, or sand; a pencil or narrow dibble.

There are three keys to a successful softwood cutting. First, choose growth that is entirely or mostly this season's growth ("softwood"). You'll have the best luck finding appropriate stems on plants that you pruned hard the year before, because after a year they are generating a fresh flush of succulent new growth. Second, take a nice long cutting, up to ten inches (25cm) long if possible. Longer branches have more energy that can be channeled into forming a new plant. Third, cut at an angle, so there's more surface area for roots to form.

Bring your pile of cuttings into your shed and array them on the bench. Remove any flowers and all but the top leaves. Make a better angled cut at the base, if need be. Then place them in a jar of water for an hour or more so they plump up as much as possible.

Meanwhile, fill the pots with a quick-draining medium, such as vermiculite, perlite, or a mixture of the two (sand also suffices, but since it is not sterile, disease can strike your cuttings). When you're ready, first dip the cut end briefly in some rooting powder and tap off any excess. Prepare holes with the dibble and gently insert each cutting. Raise the cuttings in a warm, humid spot—under mist in a greenhouse is ideal, but homemade systems consisting of bottom heat (from heating cables) and plastic tenting also work.

ELECTRICITY

Power inside your potting shed is convenient, but it is not essential. With it, you can go in at night or on a dark day and switch on a light. (You could even indulge in a porch light outside above the door.) The true gardening uses are few, but nice: with power, you can have a refrigerator for pre-chilling bulbs and stratifying seeds, and you can plug in heating cables for starting seeds. However, the latter application may be short-lived, because, as you know, little plants need light, and a shed is not a greenhouse. Finally, if you ever have occasion to use power tools—an electric screwdriver, a drill, and so on—you'll have a handy place to plug them in.

What electricity does is provide comfort. A few strategically located outlets will allow you all sorts of possibilities, from plugging in a fan on hot days to running a space heater on chilly days to listening to a radio to setting up a coffeepot or teapot.

Opposite: If your shed's location is naturally a bit shady or secluded, lighting may be necessary. Installing the wiring and outlets is generally a job best left to an electrical contractor.

As you ponder this decision, realize that it is sometimes a hassle to install electricity postconstruction, because wiring ought to be run inside a wall before the Sheetrock or paneling is added. If the interior of your shed is going to be rustic (that is, it won't have interior walls) and you decide to wire it in the future, the electrician will have to "box" the power points safely (you'll probably have to move or remove everything in the shed while the electrician works). Yes, just as with plumbing, running electrical wiring is better left to the professionals. If you really know what you are doing, and you only mean to utilize existing wiring from your home—which is adjacent or sharing a wall—perhaps you could do it yourself.

However, if your potting shed is a distance from the house, you must hire a licensed electrician to do the work. It's not just a matter of safely running protected (waterproof or armored cable) wires; the wiring of a separate circuit may be required. If you happen to have existing outdoor wiring, servicing a swimming pool for instance, perhaps the electrician can tap into that system. Again, don't try to do this yourself!

ALTERNATIVES TO ELECTRICITY

A little creativity will give you some of the benefits of electrical power without any wiring; just keep safety in mind! Battery-operated lights or lanterns are an option. Kerosene or camping lanterns should be used with great care—you don't want to start another Chicago fire!

If you're desperate for a fan or heater, in a pinch you can temporarily run one of those long, orange outdoor extension cords from the nearest outlet to your shed. Just be sure to disconnect it and roll it up when it's time to close up the shed and go back in the house. An ice chest can hold cool drinks, though it isn't very practical for gardening uses such as stratifying seeds or pre-chilling bulbs. Finally, there's no reason you can't brew your coffee or tea piping hot inside, pour it into a thermos, bring it out with you, and perch it on a handy shelf.

Sharp Edges

Finally consolidating your tool collection in the shelter of your potting shed may cause you to notice that the spade, hoe, or hedge clippers could benefit from a little attention. Having a good workspace at last may put you in the spirit. Remember, a dull tool isn't just annoying—it causes extra stress and effort on your part, does its job poorly, and may damage plant stems or roots by mashing or tearing them.

**Materials you will need:
a vise grip (if possible, mount it on the end of your potting bench or table); a single-cut, ten-inch (25cm) "bastard" file (double-cut files are for really heavy work—a ten-inch file is a comfortable size for most hands).**

The key to restoring a sharp cutting edge to a dull tool is to restore the original shiny bevel. Digging tools like shovels and trowels have single-bevel edges, usually about 35 to 40 degrees and hopefully still detectable once the tool is cleaned up. Grip both ends of the file and use a diagonal "toe to heel" motion, pushing away from your body. Don't bear down too hard, and don't drag the file back over your work. When you're done, you may run a couple quick swipes back the other way to eliminate any "feather" that formed.

Pruning tools, from loppers to clippers, are easier to sharpen if you take them apart first. For these, you will want to use a finer-grade ("second cut" or "smooth cut") file.

Decorating the Exterior

Whether your shed is homegrown or prefabricated, once it is erected, it is great fun to embellish the outside of it. It might be safe to say that gardeners, more than most home hobbyists, are sensitive to design and attractive presentation—and this structure, after all, is now a part of your garden. Just one caveat: if you make it really bright or appealing, it may steal the show from your garden and become an unwitting focal point.

PAINT AND TRIM

There are countless ways to decorate the walls, roof, and even windows and eaves of your shed.

Paints and stains are practical, as well as decorative, because they act as wood preservatives. Here are some ideas:

• Paint the door and trim a separate color.

• Paint the shed in a color that harmonizes with the adjacent garden. Even so-called neutral colors come in a fun range of choices, from sage green to café-au-lait tan to softest primrose yellow.

• If you are artistic, or have an artistic friend (or want to pay someone), how about trompe l'oeil? Imagine a scene that looks like a pleasant path leading off to the mountains or a lake; or a colorful rendition of your "dream" perennial border, giving the illusion

Putting your personal mark on the exterior of your new shed is great fun. You can do a lot with paint, from attractive trim colors to stenciling to trompe l'oeil. Or you can hang swags, wreaths, signs, or tools.

that the bloom is never off the rose; or some whimsical rabbits or curious deer (faux garden pests are permissible). The possibilities are endless.

A cottage-like, or almost Hansel-and-Gretel, character can be instantly conferred on a potting shed that has been embellished with gingerbread trim. The signature swirls and flourishes can be made of the same type of wood as the shed, or even simple outdoor plywood planks; some home-supply stores offer precut lengths, and all you have to do is get them cut to size and bring them home and attach them. Install them along the roof lines or around the door and windows, and leave them plain or paint them white or in bright colors.

Ways to add character to your shed include using "gingerbread" detailing along the roof line (opposite) and mounting pretty stained glass windows or doors (opposite and right), perhaps salvaged from another structure. While you can clean, repair, and paint these embellishments, sometimes they have a nice rustic charm when left in their original form.

A RUSTIC SHED

Perhaps you want the outside of your shed to slip quietly into the background of your garden, with little fuss or fanfare. Savvy siting may be on your side if mature or lush-growing plants are already embracing it or will in due course.

Depending on the type of wood, you still ought to give the shed a coat of something that extends its life, even if it's a neutral or brown stain. If you want to train a disguising vine up the side but not call attention to the support, try a twig or brown-colored trellis.

Curing Onions

These popular roots need to be "cured" (properly dried) to assure good flavor and a long life in storage. Simply pulling them out and braiding their lax foliage alone won't do the trick; they'll look nice for a time, but most will rot.

Materials you will need: a rake, a spading fork, a screen or rack, sharp scissors, storage bins.

Begin the process in the garden, late in the season, by knocking over already floppy tops with a hoe. Don't water their area again. They will now begin drying in the ground, most critically at their necks, which seals off the bulbs from possible invasion by pests or fungi.

Upon harvesting, lay the onions on their sides on a screen and keep them there for about a week. Don't remove the foliage and don't crowd them. Place the screen in a bright but well-ventilated spot, perhaps astride a lawn chair or wheelbarrow for better air circulation. Move the rack indoors (in your shed) at night and when rain threatens.

Finally, trim off the tops with scissors, but don't cut flush. (Of course, leave a few if you want to make braids.) Store them in single layers in boxes or bins, in a cool (but never freezing), dry place—perhaps a corner of your potting shed.

There are dozens of different types of onions, and all are relatively easy to grow. Cure them properly and you can enjoy flavorful onions all winter long.

In addition to or instead of paint, you can have fun decorating with all sorts of other things, some garden-themed, some not.

• Hang tools—a collection of rakes, say—at staggered intervals and heights. (But don't hang anything with sharp edges!)

• Mount a few baskets or just one on the door. Tuck in some pretty dried flowers.

• Get some ceramic tiles spelling your name or your pet name for your new hideaway, and attach them to the front of the shed at eye level.

• Hang "found" objects or replicas of them, such as old horseshoes, vintage license plates, and funky weather vanes.

• Fly the flag of your choice, patriotic or decorative, or a colorful windsock.

• Shop around for a handsome but weatherproof outdoor thermometer and mount it near the door so you can glance at it going and coming. Some of the gardening catalogs have charming ones.

• Tuck a decorative and/or practical birdhouse up in the eaves.

• Add the magic of sound: hang some wind chimes out front.

DECORATING WITH PLANTS

One great way to integrate your potting shed into your garden is to add plants. And integrating is a good idea, lest the building stand off and aloof from the garden it is meant to

If you're a collector, the outside walls (or inside walls, space permitting) of the shed are great places to mount displays. Among the many items that are fun to hang are vintage basins, old tools, license plates, baskets, and signs. Ideally, they should have a "gardening feel" or fit in with your shed's character and the adjacent landscaping.

serve, or become, as warned above, a focal point that dominates the attention of visitors or makes a jarring impression on them.

• If you have windows, mount window boxes. Paint them to match the shed or leave them unfinished and let their contents provide the color. Fill them with vibrant flowers or lush

While you are sure to get absorbed in indoor projects when you own a shed, give yourself—or a visitor—an inviting spot to sit down and relax, perhaps to enjoy a cup of coffee or iced tea.

foliage, or both, and don't hesitate to make changes as the mood strikes.

• Plant a couple of flowering shrubs or well-trimmed evergreens on either side of the door, in the ground or in pots.

• Make a planting bed or set out some planter boxes along the front or sides of the building.

• Planters, urns, or pots stationed along the sides or at just the corners of the structure are also good devices for welcoming the shed to the garden.

• Is there a spot that could host a trellis or at least a rigging of hooks and wires? Just remember, set any support a few inches away from the wall, not flush against it, to give whatever vine you plant some air circulation, as well as to preserve the side of your building.

• Hang wicker baskets or moss baskets filled with flowers, herbs, foliage plants, or whatever you like. If there is not much of an overhang, just get big, sturdy hooks.

Outside decor need not be attached to the exterior walls. A simple plant stand or stool can show off a welcoming array of flowering plants or knickknacks.

Reviving Overwintered Cannas

Gardeners in areas with cold winters often enjoy growing tender plants, even though they know they must dig them up each autumn. Cannas are one glorious example. When you dig up the tubers in the autumn, avoid the temptation to divide them, no matter how big they are. Instead, store them whole in small plastic bags of damp sand or soil, in a cool, dark place (perhaps not the potting shed, if you expect freezing weather).

**Materials you will need:
a sharp knife, some pots, potting soil, the stored canna tubers.**

One day in late spring, bring the plastic bags to the potting table and empty out the contents for inspection. Discard any tubers that are shriveled, dried out, or rotten. Cut up the remaining ones into good-size pieces, with an eye on each, where new growth will generate. After cutting, let them dry overnight. The next day, pot them an inch or two (2.5 or 5cm) below the soil mix's surface, water well, and give them sun and warmth. Soon fresh new growth will make its debut. After your garden's soil has warmed up and the danger of frost is past, you may transplant the new baby cannas out into the garden.

A PATH TO THE DOOR

In the interest of integrating your potting shed into the garden, it is also advisable to create some sort of approach. It can be as simple as a few steps run out from the door—use stones if you have stones elsewhere in your landscape or a rock garden; use bricks if some of your beds are edged in brick; use lumber rounds if your garden is more rustic; and so on.

If you have a grander approach in mind and have made a concerted effort from the start to incorporate your potting shed as an element of your garden's overall design, a path is in order. It may be as informal as a meandering gravel, bark-dust, or flagstone path, or as formal as a paved walkway (bordered in plantings) whose clear ultimate destination is the shed. Either way, a few quick tips are necessary.

• Visualize the planned path before you install anything; lay it out with some lengths of rope or hoses.

• Start at the door and work outward.

• If you're working with stones or pavers, lay the largest or most handsome one right at the door first, then turn your attention to the rest of the project.

• Install landscaping after the fact, bearing in mind that eager growers will need to be reined in occasionally. An alternative is to use potted plants that can be shifted around or replaced when they cease blooming.

Some paths lead directly to the shed door (left), while others take a few turns along the way (opposite). The advantage of the former is that your destination is clear and obvious, but there is more privacy and a sense of anticipation with a meandering approach.

Transplanting Seedlings

Pricking out and graduating delicate little seedlings to new pots is a pleasant chore when you have a potting shed. The potting bench or table allows you plenty of elbowroom, and all you need now is good light and time enough to work carefully without rushing.

Materials you will need: a small implement such as a pencil or fork, a sufficient amount of small pots, new potting soil.

Here are a few tips to keep in mind as you carefully lift and transfer each tiny plant:
• Let the flat dry out a bit before transplanting day so the roots are more easily separated from their growing medium.
• Never pull a seedling out by the stem, which may bruise or snap it. If you must tug, grab a little leaf.
• When you are finished, water the pots well. Watering from above should be done gingerly so you don't dislodge the little plant. Alternatively, set the pots in a shallow tray of water and let them soak up what they need.

When you have a potting place, you will find yourself taking on—and truly enjoying—more elaborate potting and transplanting projects. Everything you need, plus ample space to work in, is now on hand.

Furnishing the Interior

It's moving-in day, the moment you've been waiting for! Just as with moving into a new house or apartment, you need to take the biggest objects in first and set them up. Then change your mind about where they belong if need be. That most likely means maneuvering the potting bench or table into place before anything else. Be especially sure that you like the lighting—at various times of the day—because seeing your work is going to be key.

After you are happy with the placement of your large items, load in your storage receptacles, pot collection (at last, it has a home!), and various tools. Haul in the supplies and fill bins or drawers. Hang up any pictures, posters, charts, or decorations. After you've lived with the setup for some time, you're sure to make modifications. But nothing beats the exhilarating feeling of standing in the middle of the little room, twirling on your heel, and admiring your new domain.

STORAGE IDEAS

Storing gardening tools and supplies inside isn't just convenient or cosmetic. Outdoor life or storage in a damp garage is bad for them. Tools rust, terra-cotta pots deteriorate when subjected to wet and freezing

Savvy organization will reduce clutter at the outset and help you keep track of what you have. A clay pot collection, for example, can be stored in a variety of ways. Stacks are fine, so long as they don't get too high. Smaller pots can be arrayed on shelves, while larger, dirty, or damaged ones can be stowed under benches.

weather, plastic pots and tarps break down when exposed to long periods of sunlight, and bags of loose soil, amendments, and fertilizer can become as hard as cement when exposed to dampness.

Under the protective cover of the shed, every gardener has his or her favorite receptacles and cubbyholes, but following you'll find a few nifty ideas that have worked well for others.

• If you have lots of clay pots, lay them, nested, on their sides. If you stack them one atop another, you'll soon have a precarious tower.

• Keep plastic bags sealed with twist ties or rubber bands. Keep bins and barrels covered.

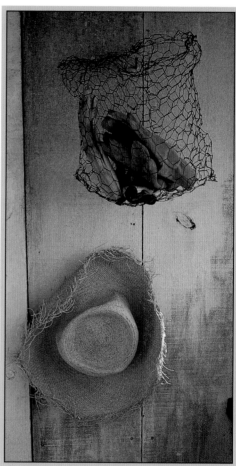

Above: Plenty of hooks at eye or hand level allow you to keep items handy yet out of the way. Left: Probably the best way to store similar-size pots is on their sides. This way you can make longer stacks without worrying about them tumbling over and shattering.

Everything in its place: plenty of hooks, nooks, and shelving keeps a shed gratifyingly neat and orderly. After all, a big reason you wanted a shed was so that you could find things without the annoyance of rooting around in jumbled piles or various locations.

- Tuck the working edges of larger tools, such as hoes, rakes, push brooms, and cultivators, over the exposed rim of the top of the wall. Or give each one its own hook.
- Mount a basket or old letter box near the door for stowing your garden gloves, so you can grab them quickly as you pass by.

- Line shelves with smaller and attractive pots. That way, they'll be handy if you need them. In the meantime, you may find them useful for holding smaller supplies, such as plant tags, tape, pens, or twine.
- Bring in a small file cabinet if you have a corner for it. You can store seed, nursery orders and packing lists, catalogs, and magazines. Or take out the file supports and use a drawer for hand tools or small pots.
- Old milk crates or wooden wine boxes (ask at your local wine store; often these boxes are just thrown out) make good homes for seed packets and envelopes.

A SMALL LIBRARY

Although you may have an extensive collection of gardening books indoors, from Henry Mitchell's essays to hefty American or Royal Horticultural Society reference books, consider moving some of these out to the potting shed. Not all of them, of course—shed life may be hard on the finer-looking or more treasured ones (damp air, dust, and the gardener's dirty hands soon take away their luster). Take just a few of the ones you refer to most often, either for information or inspiration.

Erect a shelf for them, preferably handy to the potting bench so you can grab one if you need to answer a quick question or double-check some information. Be sure it's a strong shelf that can take the weight, and if need be, provide ends or bookends to keep books from cascading onto the floor.

Your shed "library" might also include your favorite seed and nursery catalogs, again for handy reference, or magazines that you subscribe to, though they are not always helpful at the spur of the moment unless you can lay your hands on an annual index (usually printed in the year-end issue). Put them in a box or bin, because growing piles soon slump and slide. Alternatively, stash them in a small file cabinet.

One last item: add a cup or jar of pens (including a yellow highlighter) and pencils and some yellow sticky notes to the bookshelf. Its contents are sure to come in handy.

Left: Now is your chance to consolidate or keep on hand reference materials that you use often. Set aside a place for your favorite gardening books. Opposite: Imagine how nice it will be to sit at your potting bench carefully filling out your seed orders. Afterwards, you can put everything away—catalogs, notes, lists, canceled checks, and the like—in an appointed spot.

A GARDENING JOURNAL

To some gardeners, the most indispensable tool is not the trowel or the hose—it's a gardening journal. Your new potting shed signals an exciting new commitment to your garden and to being more organized. If you don't already keep a journal, now is the ideal time to start one—and to leave it in the shed so you can make entries right on the spot.

The best argument for keeping a garden journal is that you forget things; you think you will remember when you sowed the hellebores or cabbage, or the name of that new salvia, or exactly where you planted the trout lilies, or when that rosebush stopped blooming. But you forget. The mind can hold only so much information, and in this age of computers and calculators and other conveniences, perhaps our minds jettison even more information, having lost the habit or need of holding it.

A journal can be highly organized, with shopping lists and germination and bloom time data, and chances to juxtapose last year's information with this year's. Or it can be a diary of sorts, written in daily or almost daily. It can be a store-bought "blank book" or one designed and intended for gardening records. Some gardeners, however, prefer a spiral-bound type, which has the advantage of lying flat if you want to leave it open or consult it while your hands are full.

Formal or informal, a gardener's journal quickly becomes personalized. You may tuck in snapshots and clippings from magazines and catalogs, or paperclip in notes to yourself on scraps of paper. If it lives in the potting shed, it is also bound to become dirt-smeared—in other words, well used and well loved.

One important tip: date every entry, and don't forget to add the year! This key piece of information may turn out to be the most useful, time and again. Thumbing back later can be a pleasure in and of itself. The biggest benefit of a garden journal, many say, is that it teaches you to record—and trust—your own observations and therefore to become more intimate with your own garden, instead of always relying on memory and reference books. Add your journal to the library shelf, tuck it into the top drawer of your potting bench, or hang it by its spiral wires on a handy hook—it's wise to always store it in the same spot.

Chapter Three

Potting Corners

Not everyone has the space, need, or resources for something as big as a potting shed. But that doesn't mean you can't enjoy the genuine pleasure and gratifying efficiency that a designated place offers. With a little planning and creativity, you can set up a lovely "potting corner" that will serve your needs. Depending on where you locate it, there may be room for expansion (if you wish to add more storage bins, for example), plus you'll have the flexibility to pick up and move everything to a better or more elaborate spot later.

Siting

When space in or around your home is limited, choosing the right spot is key. You need a place that is sufficiently out of the way of household traffic so curious pets, exploring children, and nongardening adults won't invade it or stumble across it in the course of their daily activities. A little elbowroom is also nice—you don't want to stuff your work area into a crowded corner of the garage or basement where you have to move or climb over stuff each time you want to use it.

There is a reason potting corners are called "corners"; the best location often seems to be one that has walls on two sides. This effectively protects your supplies and work from household traffic or the encroachment of other projects set up by you or the people you live with. Tools and supplies cannot be shoved to the left or the right, or back, when they are secured in a corner. Setting up in an actual corner also permits you to make the spot seem a little bit more permanent, because you can erect shelves, hang tools, and add decorations—or even a "to do" chalkboard—on one or both walls.

You also need good light, especially if the appointed spot is indoors. Setting up on a table or bench under a window is appealing, because gardeners, perhaps more than most hobbyists, love natural light. If the window overlooks your yard, you are in luck, because seeing the garden will motivate you. If the light from a window is insufficient, or if you expect to use the area on dark days or in the evening or early morning (likely possibilities),

Any sheltered spot with some shelving and a table can be converted into a potting area. You can fine-tune the features and add amenities as necessary.

artificial light is a must. A lightbulb or fluorescent light source, preferably mounted directly overhead or across from you, is best. A stand-alone desk lamp or a small or clip-on fixture are other options.

Also choose a place that is adjacent to or not far from a water source, because so many gardening projects seem to require water (plus you'll want to wash your hands when you are finished).

Bring water to your potting corner by running out some piping and installing a spigot. A hose will extend your reach as needed; be sure it has a trigger.

POTTING CORNERS ➤ 87

POTTING PLACE PROJECT

Dividing a Houseplant

Although you can divide many houseplants any time they appear to be outgrowing their quarters, late winter or early spring is best, because the plants are generally dormant then, but are poised to burst into fresh growth.

**Materials you will need:
pots (choose ones somewhat smaller than the one that the big, overgrown houseplant currently occupies), a stiff scrub brush, water, bleach, soilless potting mix, a bucket or sink, a trowel, knives.**

Prepare the new pots first, probably two or three, depending on the size of the plant. Scrub them out if necessary, and rinse them briefly in a solution of nine parts water to one part bleach to disinfect them. Dump the soil mix into a bucket, moisten it, and press some into the bottom of each new pot.

Now, extract the plant from its pot. You may need to run a knife around the inside to pry it loose. If you also whack the bottom, try not to yank on the foliage at the same time—just wiggle and ease it loose. Shake the old soil from the roots, and gently rinse them off.

To divide, tease and pry apart the root ball into natural sections, ones that have a balance of roots and foliage. If it's tough going, slice the root ball apart with a sharp knife. Discard any brown or damaged growth.

Repot the divisions in the new pots at the same level they were growing, and press additional damp potting mix in around them. Water well, and keep them in a warm spot out of direct light for a few days so they can recover.

The Work Surface

Resourceful gardeners, or those on a budget, set up terrific potting corners with minimal trouble and expense, using whatever they have on hand or can scavenge from the garage or a yard sale. There is the height of the table to be considered. Most kitchen-type tables and card tables are only about twenty-eight inches (71cm) tall, too short to work at while standing up. While you could rig something that elevates such a table to a better height (around thirty-three to thirty-eight inches [84 to 97cm] is comfortable for most people), you're better off finding or building something that suits. Tables meant for folding laundry on are good, as are certain workbenches meant for woodworkers or picture framers.

What should your work surface be made of? You can certainly cover something that is rough or difficult to clean with a plastic tablecloth, contact paper, or a layer of

Above: the simplest potting or trimming tasks can be done on a small table. Cover the surface with an easy-to-clean vinyl tablecloth or some contact paper. Opposite: You don't need to have an official "potting table"—any tall table at least two feet (60cm) deep will fit the bill. Set it under a window for natural light, and let a wall act as a backsplash.

papers, but it's also nice to have a surface where this is not necessary.

Wood: Even with the modest demands of potting and tending plants indoors, wood surfaces are still prone to warping or becoming dirty over time. Your best bet is a smooth wood, perhaps with a protective coating of preservative or paint. Otherwise, you should get in the habit of brushing off, then sponging clean, the surface after every use.

Plastic: A plastic tabletop or bench is a cinch to clean. The main disadvantage is that repeated use causes staining; and if you use sharp cutting tools (such as a knife while making cuttings), you'll nick or lacerate the surface.

Metal: Metal tables look great on day one, and aren't hard to clean, but they eventually show wear (scratches, rust, pockmarks). Also, if they are at all flimsy, they are difficult to work on.

Indoor Potting Corners

Choice or necessity may cause you to set up in the basement, in the garage, or even at the far end of the dining room, kitchen, or laundry room. Walk around the house and scout out good spots. Try clearing

Above: At its most basic, all a potting corner really needs is a water source and a work surface. Right: A metal work surface is a cinch to clean—a quick swipe of the sponge does the trick. Opposite: The key to a successful indoor potting area is clearing it of all other uses; make its purpose clear to the nongardeners in your home.

DECORATE YOUR INDOOR HAVEN

Just for fun, you should dress up your potting corner. Here are a few ideas to help you make your potting space comfortable and homey:

....

• Cover the work surface or table with a pretty plastic tablecloth or contact paper. It'll be easy to clean.
• If you are situated near a window, make or buy some new curtains—perhaps ones with flowers or a garden motif.
• If the window has a sill or there's space on an adjacent shelf (install a shelf, if you like), line it with a few potted plants, attractive pots, or vases of dried or silk flowers. Or go out to the garden and pick a bouquet or a few sprigs before you start to work. Of course, don't set these things on your work surface, where they will just get in the way or get knocked over.
• Mount hooks on the wall and hang a pretty wreath or dried bouquets of flowers or herbs.
• Hang up one or several pictures (garden photographs or botanical drawings, perhaps) or helpful reference charts (sometimes garden magazines include bonus posters featuring useful information).

---

out the area first, perhaps wedging in a small table if no other work surface is present—and leaving it alone for a few days. This test will allow you to decide if you like the spot and if other members of your household are likely to respect it.

If you think it will be necessary, protect the spot when you're not using it by tossing a tarp or cloth over everything, or by erecting screens or other physical barriers around it.

Of course, a tarp is fine in the basement or garage, but it will appear unsightly if your potting corner is to be set up in a living area. If you've chosen the dining room or family room for your potting place, consider giving the room a garden theme, making your potting things part of the decor.

If your chosen spot has poor light, move in a lamp or have an electrician install a new light overhead or nearby. If this isn't possible,

A potting place shouldn't be for just work and storage. Arrange it with care, then add in extras, such as lighting and seating, that are pretty as well as practical. Give it personality by decorating with wreaths, swags, pictures, flowering plants (light permitting), and knickknacks.

try putting a higher wattage bulb in the existing light source or redirecting its beam.

An area under a window, in a basement, for example, may have the small problem of poor insulation. It seems many of these windows are not airtight, and on a winter's day, when you are sowing seeds, the frosty air will make your fingers cold and less agile. Tape or seal the window gaps, or put up an insulating shade or curtain and see if that helps (of course, then you'll need an alternative light source).

If the area seems "close" or humid, crack the nearest window or run a fan. If you are adjacent to the washing machine and dryer, work when they are not operating so your senses won't be drubbed by their noise, vibrations, and smell.

Last but not least, you likely will find yourself dependent on a sink for water. Utility and laundry sinks seem to have larger, more forgiving drains (they often empty directly into your home's waste pipes), but a kitchen or bathroom sink or bathtub can become clogged if you continually wash potting mix down it. Use a strainer and empty it before letting the water out.

Outdoor Potting Corners

Gardeners who lack indoor space, prefer to work in the fresh air, or are blessed with a mild climate have the option of setting up outside. One advantage to this approach is that you'll have plenty of light and ventilation. Postproject cleanups may be easier, too, as you brush soil mix and other amendments off one end of your potting table or gather them up and casually broadcast them in the garden or on the compost pile.

However, an outdoor potting corner is harder to protect—from the elements, other people, and pets. Assuming you don't consider the spot temporary, it must be in an out-of-the-way location. Get shade and shelter from wind under an awning, a vine-covered pergola, or perhaps an ample beach umbrella. When you're not there, throw a tarp or blanket over the entire works, or cover it with boards or large sheets of cardboard anchored with a few rocks or bricks. A covering is not especially pretty, true, but it is necessary to keep out the elements and intruders (human as well as animal). Of course, if the appearance really bothers you, with a little effort you can always devise something that you consider to be more attractive.

Outdoor locations also have the advantage of being accessible to the water hose, which you can drag over if its spigot is some distance away. Alternatively, fill some watering cans and set them by your potting corner so they're ready when you need them.

Above: An impromptu spot can be set up outside on a nice day; bring along just the tools and supplies you will need. Opposite: Even a set of wide shelves may serve admirably in a small potting corner. The surface at waist-height acts as a worktable, while upper shelves keep potting necessities within easy reach.

OUTDOOR SITES FOR POTTING CORNERS

A little pondering will usually turn up a good out-of-the-way spot for a potting venture. Here are a few areas you might consider:
....
• The corner of a balcony or patio, one wall of which is the house
• The least-used corner of a deck or the space under a pergola or awning
• An old table or picnic table, wedged against the house or garage, or moved to a back corner of the yard against the fence

A TEMPORARY POTTING CORNER

You may prefer—or have no choice about—making your potting corner temporary. This means retrieving your supplies and tools every time you want to start a project and returning them to storage when you are done. Make sure, then, that you have plenty of good storage receptacles, and stash them neatly and in an easily accessible location.

The disadvantage of a temporary spot, of course, is that setting up and breaking down can become a hassle, particularly in the case of more elaborate projects. However, there are a few advantages.

• You can set up anywhere you want, indoors or outside.
• You can work in different places, depending on the requirements of the project at hand (near the sink or hose when you are transplanting small plants; in good light when you need to clean or sharpen a tool).
• You can gather only what you need for a given project, rather than being surrounded by (and perhaps crowded by) extraneous tools or supplies.
• Valuable space is not taken up, because a potting corner laid out for work takes up more area than the same supplies stashed away in storage.

Choose an out-of-the-way nook for your outdoor potting place so you will be able to work out of the path of traffic and, when you are not there, the area can remain undisturbed.

Ways to Keep It Neat and Efficient

When you stock a potting corner with supplies and tools, space is obviously at much more of a premium than it is for someone who has a potting shed. Just as chefs set up their kitchens so they can operate efficiently, so should you try to save yourself steps and the inconveniences of going over or around some things to get to others.

PROPER PLACES

Making certain that everything in your corner—from tools to gloves to potting mix—has its own place is the secret to working efficiently. Proper storage also ensures that supplies are out of the way until you need them, preventing unwanted clutter from accumulating.

Hooks: You can have anything from a single hook for a work apron or a pair of gloves to a series of hooks or dowels for an array of tools. Towel racks or coatracks with several pegs are often worthwhile; mount them above your worktable but within arm's reach for convenience.

Small and stackable bins: Potting corner owners have less space and therefore should buy supplies in smaller quantities or store them elsewhere. A tub filled with soil mix or perlite, for example, should be small enough to fit under or next to the work surface. A lid on the tub will help keep out moisture and intruders, and may allow you

As in a well-planned, well-appointed kitchen, creative and practical storage is what makes a potting place a joy to use. You can always modify or customize over time.

to stack other similar-size containers on top of it.

Other containers: Use as many containers or receptacles as possible, from small clay pots chock-full of pens to pencil boxes stuffed with plant markers to bags or boxes full of stakes. Be creative! This storage system allows you to move things around until you find the very best spot for them—so, eventually, you can simply reach for what you need with hardly a look.

Shelves: Space and site permitting, sturdy shelving is a real asset to a potting corner. Down low, shelves provide storage for heavier or bulkier items. Up high, at eye level or within reach of your outstretched hand, they allow you to array often-used tools, such as the trowel, knives, and "seedling helpers" (see page 41), or simply to perch a mug of coffee. You may also be able to indulge in a few decorative items on shelves, just to make the corner feel more homey.

Drawers: A clever potting corner idea is to press an old dresser into service. The top can be your work surface (or not, if you have a better tabletop nearby), and the drawers can hold all manner of tools and supplies. Other ways to get the benefits of drawers is to co-opt an old handyman's table or file cabinet and fill it with whatever will fit.

SORTING AND LABELING

Part of being well organized in a small area is grouping together similar items. Do this as you set up for the first time, and make mod-

Opposite: Group similar-size tools so you'll have an easier time finding what you need when you need it—reason alone to have a potting area in the first place. Right: Space permitting, tuck in extra shelving where you can—it may be useful for storage or as a staging area, or both.

ifications as you go if need be. Stick small items in small containers, put sharp items (such as knives and pruners) together, and organize amendments according to how often you dip into them.

A system of color-coding works for some gardeners. All fertilizers go in yellow tubs; all perennial seeds go in the red plastic toolbox; all vegetable seeds in the green; and so on.

Labeling is always wise. True, it may be overly fussy to label a jar "plant markers" when you can very well see what it contains, but bins with lids and drawers should be tagged. Envelopes of seeds should be marked, too, and these labels should include dates so you can keep track of freshness. If you get creative with the labels (using canning jar labels with decorative borders, for instance), your potting corner will be even prettier.

POTTING PLACE PROJECT

Repotting an Orchid

An orchid needs to be repotted when its roots begin to quest out and away from the container; there's a profusion of pseudobulbs without foliage or flowering stalks; and the potting mixture appears sodden, draining poorly. Wait until the plant is not flowering to reduce stress. To avoid the risk of infection, be sure to continually dip your cutting knife in rubbing alcohol to sterilize it.

**Materials you will need:
dampened fir bark, a knife, pruners,
rubbing alcohol.**

Gently extract the root ball from the pot. Tease it apart, shaking and picking off remnants of the old mix. Cut off any roots that are damaged or blackened. Also remove any unproductive pseudobulbs.

To repot, carefully place the rootstock in the new pot (or a clean used one), with the oldest, fattest part of it wedged against one side. This allows it room to elongate outward with fresh new growth. Sprinkle new fir bark below and around it until the plant sits securely in place. Temporarily set the orchid in a sheltered spot out of direct light, mist it daily, and watch for signs of new growth—which comes usually within a month or two of repotting.

Group tools and supplies according to function—keep all the digging implements together, for example. Favorite items should be the most accessible. Naturally, you may wish to modify the arrangements over time.

Special Products for the Potting Corner

Just as retail garden centers and catalog merchants have noticed and tried to cater to the trend of smaller outdoor gardens in recent years, so have they been trying to better serve the indoor gardener. Some of the new products are admittedly optional, but they are often clever or helpful and perhaps worthy of your investment.

Note that these items are, for the most part, quite portable, which means you can easily move them around within your potting corner as you experiment with the best way to use them. And you can change where you work, perhaps moving into better light for certain projects or taking a whole project outside for a change if it's a nice day (see A Temporary Potting Corner on page 96).

Potting cart: This is the latest trend in potting corner "technology," and a good one —with plenty of work and storage space— may be just about all you need. The best ones come with sliding bins or drawers, movable shelves, molded tool slots, and a removable sink. You can easily spend quite a bit of cash. If you're poised to invest in one, also consider a more traditional potting bench, as described in detail in Chapter 4.

Important: Some potting carts are meant to be stationary, so you just set yours up where you want it to stay and load in everything. Others come equipped with wheels so you can scoot them around, even right out into the garden if you wish, and roll them into storage when not in use (look out, though—if you tip up a two-wheeler like a dolly, a mess ensues).

Potting tidy: This is basically a modified tray, with a lip all around to keep your potting project confined within and thus keep your work area free of messy soil or water spills. That's the theory, anyway. The smaller ones are hard to work with, however. It may not make sense to put the bin or bag of potting mix inside, so spills are still possible as you scoop back and forth. Also, the design can cause you to awkwardly tuck in your wrists and elbows. So buy a potting tidy that's an ample size (at least two feet [60cm] across). Depth back to the backsplash is usu-ally a little less (typically twenty inches [50cm]), which works fine. A plus is that a potting tidy is easy to clean—just rinse it off when you're finished. At $25 or less, this product is a nice investment.

Potter's island: A nifty, self-contained workstation, about two feet (60cm) in diameter, this plastic tray is worth considering. The round shape and small size make it possible for you to turn the island as you work, useful when tamping soil evenly into a pot or giving a little topiary a haircut, for instance. Some come with a raised,

A potting "caddy" or cart offers several appealing benefits: it's well designed, it's versatile, and it may even be portable so you can try it out in different locations.

You can buy or customize items that make potting projects easier and more efficient. Above, left: A potting tray or "tidy" is just the right size and shape for smaller jobs. Above, right: A divided tray or drawer is a handy receptacle for reducing clutter on the work surface.

flat-topped platform mounted in the middle (like an overturned pot that doesn't slip), so you can set a potting project in progress atop it while letting soil sift away, water drain off, or prunings fall down—for later cleanup. These trays are quite affordable and can be bought through specialty suppliers.

Watering wand: Assuming you have a faucet nearby, a small attachment that reaches to your potting corner is a great convenience. Naturally, you want one with a trigger so you can control what you use. Check greenhouse suppliers for the best selection. Deluxe models (with coiling hose or adjustable nozzles) can get expensive, but you can certainly get an adequate one for a reasonable price.

Storage caddy: These are small buckets or baskets that enhance the organization of a small area. Consider wire ones, which are light and attractive, for holding pots; plastic ones (like janitors use for cleaning supplies) for holding tools or jars of plant food; or wooden "trugs" or shallow baskets for stash-

ing often-used tools or gloves. Prices start at a couple of dollars but range higher for more decorative choices.

Tool belt: It can be one designed for a carpenter, one meant for gardeners, or even a "fanny pack" shifted around to the front. The idea is to strap it on while you work and load it with items, such as pruners or markers, that you need constantly during the project at hand. This frees your hands and opens up your workspace. When it's not in use, hang it from a hook or store it. The price varies, depending on what you choose, but an inexpensive tool belt or fanny pack certainly can be had.

A table with leaves: Before you settle for an old card table or laundry table, consider setting up your potting corner with something expandable. Small eat-in-kitchen–style tables have leaves that flip up and anchor in place, or can be hooked on. Suddenly, your potting corner can become a little larger—permanently, or as needed. Price varies.

Sawhorse plant stand: These are often three-shelf affairs, with each successively higher shelf narrower than the last so that bigger items can go on the lower shelves without, as it were, banging their heads. Usually marketed as a way to display potted plants, such a stand might also be pressed into service in a potting corner as a way to store various supplies. Depending on the size, quality, and stability, you can spend as much as you would for a lower-end potting bench. Or save money and customize by making your own.

Bucket seat: Although intended for use outdoors, where the durable construction and lid provide the gardener with a low seat to perch on, this innovative product makes good storage sense on its own. Most are the five-gallon size, which means you can put some potting mix or other amendment inside. The canvas tool pouch that surrounds a bucket seat can hold everything from pruners to pens, dibbles, and plant markers. Prices vary.

Grafting a Cactus

This is a fun project, handy when you want to attach one of those red or yellow cacti to a green rootstock cactus, join a slow grower to a vigorous rootstock, or experiment with pairing a columnar cactus to one with a trailing habit. The rootstock should be stout and well-rooted. Wear gloves to protect not only yourself from the sharp spines but also the knife as you work. Begin by dipping the knife blade in rubbing alcohol to sterilize it, and dip it again before each subsequent cut throughout the operation.

Materials you will need: a sharp knife, gloves, rubbing alcohol, rubber bands, cotton ball.

Neatly slice the top off the rootstock, then slice it to form a shallow point using a quick, downward motion of the knife. Then carve a matching cut in the scion piece so it will fit atop the rootstock. Align as closely as you can; a perfect fit may not be possible, but at least try to line up a portion of the cambium rings (not unlike tree rings).

Help the two pieces join by pressing them together snugly and then placing a cotton ball on top of the scion and running rubber bands over the entire project. In a few weeks, they should be operating as one plant and you can gently remove the holding materials.

Trays and flats of all kinds will find a home in a potting place. Do yourself a favor and clean them out before storing them, so you can put them to immediate use when you need them.

TWO OLD CROWS
LIVE HERE!

Chapter Four

Potting Benches

The first time you stand before an actual potting bench and run a hand across its work surface, check out the various shelves below and above, and eyeball its height in relation to yours, don't be surprised if you are consumed with a familiar feeling. Call it gardener's lust, the very same thing that happens when you heft a particularly finely crafted spade or peruse an especially comprehensive array of, say, heathers or clematis vines. All of a sudden, a potting

bench seems like an absolute necessity in your life. Once you have it home and in use for a while, you'll agree—a potting bench is not a luxury.

Like any other garden addition, this one needs an appropriate spot, and it's wise to decide where—more or less, anyway—before you go shopping. If you have a potting shed, are poised to install one, or have cleared out a corner of

a greenhouse, you had better know the dimensions so you don't buy a bench that overwhelms the space. If the bench comes preassembled (or is an artist's piece or a junk shop special—and therefore already all in one piece), size also becomes an issue because you don't want to settle on something that is impossible to get through the door. It seems people at first imagine potting benches to be smaller than they actually are, which is generally in the range of five feet (1.5m) long and three feet (1m) deep.

A good location for an alfresco potting bench is along a wall outdoors or on the least-trafficked end of a patio, deck, or terrace. Such spots work out well as long as the bench gets some shelter from sun and weather. (Alternatively, you can plan to toss a large tarp covering over it when it's not in use, much like some people do with their barbecue grills and outdoor furniture.)

If you plan to put the new potting bench inside, you might tuck it into the back of a garage that is used for storage (not for cars) or erect it in a basement or utility room. Again, take into account the item's assembled size. When deciding where to put it, consider also the issues of light, both natural and artificial, and water, discussed in the previous chapter.

THE PRICE OF A BENCH

Although you may be persuaded of your need for a potting bench, it behooves you to do plenty of shopping around. Styles, materials, quality, and therefore, prices vary widely. You can spend practically nothing if you make your own out of salvaged parts, around $200 if you buy good cedar lumber and other supplies (see Further Reading for books with plans), or anywhere between $80 and $800 if you purchase one from a gardening store or catalog.

The Design of a Potting Bench

Although it is called a "bench," a potting bench is really a worktable. The concept is very simple: it is a work surface that the gardener can belly up to comfortably, with shelves, hooks, and drawers within easy reach for tools and supplies. Once you live with your bench for a while, of course, you will find ways to make the best use of its features or to add the ones you need directly to it or nearby.

DIMENSIONS

Although taller and shorter gardeners may have to do some extra shopping around or have their potting bench custom-made, most of us can work easily with the standard design. Homemade or store-bought, of course, a bench can be customized. As noted above, most benches turn out to be broader and deeper than initially expected, but you will be grateful for all the space you can get once the bench is in use.

Length: Hold your arms out, as far as you can reach. It's about five feet (1.5m), isn't it? This is the ideal length for a potting bench, because you will be able to get at anything placed upon it, whether it's the bucket of perlite or the plant tags at the end of the top shelf. Although you're not going to stand stark still for hours as you work on some gardening project, hopefully, and you might even want to sit perched on a stool at times, the reasoning behind the standard length is that you shouldn't have to scoot around a lot.

Depth: Now hold your arms out in front of you—about two feet (60cm) or so, right? Such a depth is desirable, again, so everything is accessible. Potting benches that are

Above: Some catalogs offer ingenious potting benches that fold compactly for easy storage, yet are perfectly strong and stable when set up. **Opposite:** A metal grid lower shelf and backsplash keep clean easily, and the backsplash can be hung with S-hooks for extra storage.

A PORTABLE POTTING BENCH?

A wood potting bench is fairly heavy, and even more so once fully loaded with tools and supplies. Still, you may wish to have the option of moving it around, even if it's just to shift it aside to sweep the floor beneath it. When you first get your bench home, turn it over and mount heavy-duty castors. Use four-inch (10cm) industrial-grade ones, with brakes so the bench doesn't roll unless you want it to. For extra stability, attach six-inch (18cm) wooden blocks to the leg bottoms first, then screw in the castors. Note that all this will raise the level of the table several inches.

Above and opposite: Ideally, a bench should have a large work surface, plus a lower shelf for storing big items and a smaller upper shelf for housing tools and smaller supplies. Variations include slats on the lower shelf and extra side supports for stability.

somewhat deeper, say, three feet (1m), may be preferable, however, because you can push supplies, tools, or parts of the project-in-progress out of the way and pull them forward only as needed. If you opt for a shallower bench, you'll want a staging area or storage on an upper shelf.

Height: It's easy to calculate the best height for a work surface where you are most likely to be standing rather than sitting. Just measure one of your kitchen counters or some other worktable (a carpentry bench, or a sewing or quilting table)—any place where you often stand and work comfortably. Naturally, you want neither to stoop constantly nor to stand on your toes or on a stool. The industry standard for potting bench height seems to be between thirty-three and thirty-eight inches (84 and 97cm). The higher the work surface is, the less bending you have to do—so the less strain you place on your back. Of course, if the height is off only slightly, there are plenty of ways to make minor adjustments: you might saw an inch or two (2.5 to 5cm) off the legs to lower the bench or insert shims to raise the height.

CLEANING ROUTINE

Cleaning up after yourself isn't just for neatness, it prolongs the life of the potting bench. Get in the habit of putting everything away—your tools and supplies now have appointed storage places anyway. Then wipe down or hose off the work surface, and if warranted, dry it off. Handy cleaning supplies include:

....

- Sponges
- Small hand broom or brush
- Dustpan
- Old rags or towels

Lilies from Offsets

Accidentally or on purpose, you may discover that your lily plants form little underground "bulblets." You can deliberately dig up lily bulbs and harvest some of the scales that precede these. The original plant will be revitalized and you can propagate new small plants that eventually can be returned to the garden. Note that unlike tulips, daffodils, and even onions, lily bulbs form a series of overlapping scales, reminiscent of an artichoke. Undertake this project when the plants are not in bloom.

Materials you will need: a trowel or digging fork, fungicide, a damp towel, peat or sphagnum moss, plastic bags, and new pots.

To harvest the scales, dig down around your lily plants and snap off a few before replacing the dirt around the main plants. Take the scales to your potting bench, dust them lightly with a fungicide, and temporarily wrap them in a damp towel to prevent them from drying out. Meanwhile, prepare their plastic bags by filling each one with a few handfuls of damp moss. Insert the scales inside so that you can still see them, seal the bags, and then poke a hole or two in each for ventilation. Place them in a warm, dark place (like the laundry room) for about six weeks.

At the end of that period, you should be able to spot tiny round bulblets forming at the base of each scale. Don't pot them yet; instead, move the bags to the refrigerator for two or three months (the winter months).

Come spring, retrieve the bags and plant each bulblet, scale and all (for its food reserves), in its own pot. Once they are established, you can very carefully remove the scales at last and plant the small lilies in bigger pots or out in the garden.

EXTRA TOOL STORAGE

Potting benches provide storage for tools and supplies either above or below the work surface so that the area doesn't become cluttered. But assuming your bench isn't wedged into a tight area, you can create additional storage space by mounting a few hooks or nails off the end of the bench, on both sides if you wish. From these you can hang tools, gloves, or even a little hand broom. The items will be off your workspace, but within reach.

The dimensions of the work surface are important. It should be deep enough so that you can shove things to the back or sides if need be and wide enough so that you can spread out as you work.

WORK SURFACE

A totally flat work surface is common in store-bought potting benches, and you can certainly work with it. But it is not always best. If you have a choice, a slightly sloped potting surface is desirable. It has the advantage of permitting water to drain off instead of accumulating or pooling, and soil can be scooped or moved about easily. Ideally, the surface should slope toward you, not toward the back of the potting table (causing predictable problems of disposal, spillage, leaking, and warping). If your bench does not come designed this way, try elevating (propping up) the back legs an inch (2.5cm) or less to see if you like the idea. Alternatively, the work surface can slope toward a centrally situated drain, like some kitchen sinks do.

If you elect to have a flat area on which to work and you know you'll be using water often, consider using material other than wood, which doesn't weather moisture very well—or get in the habit of cleaning up thoroughly after every use. Otherwise, plastic, metal, and thoroughly grouted tile work are some of your alternatives.

ADDITIONAL FEATURES

Though this is not essential, many potting surfaces have low edges on three sides and not on the side at which you work. This is sensible, because you will be able to keep piles of soil from drifting off, and a nudged or pushed pot can be stopped from going overboard. To be effective, these edges should be around two to four inches (5 to 10cm) high, at least. Extra-high edges are advisable on simple potting benches that lack overhead shelves.

A backsplash—a vertical surface on the rear of the bench—is a practical way to limit spills as your work materials tend to scoot to the back of the surface. It also keeps you from soiling or damaging whatever is behind your potting area. It's a good idea, if possible, to have a backsplash that is water-repellent; with wooden benches, this means coating it with a preservative or taking a cue from household sink backsplashes and installing vinyl or another plastic there. For extra insurance, you can run a quick line of sealer or grouting where the backsplash meets the work surface.

Very basic potting benches have backsplashes that are not flush with the work surface but are basically just a supporting board across the back. Their main purpose is to serve as a backstop. At the other end of the spectrum, some commercial potting benches come with metal screening or grating in the backsplash position. This still works as a backstop, plus it's easy to clean with a spray of water.

A lower shelf is an ideal location for heavier supplies, such as potting mix; this way, you can reach down quickly and scoop out what you need while working.

A DELUXE BENCH

Your shopping research may turn up some pretty fancy options. The most expensive wooden benches can cost more than $800. For that amount of money, you have every right to expect cypress, probably the most durable, rot-resistant, and beautiful wood available.

Features may include:
....
• Quality construction; steel hardware and fittings that are ample, for support and strength, but concealed from view for the sake of attractiveness
• A sink or chute in the work surface (complete with a lift-out door so you can use the entire table when the sink is not needed)
• Ample upper and lower shelves, perhaps adjustable
• A peg-board for tools, perhaps with movable Shaker pegs

Houseplants from Leaf Cuttings

This propagation method is used widely by nurseries, and there's no reason why a home gardener can't succeed with it. Houseplants that reproduce very well in this way include African violets, begonias (Rex and regular ones), and gloxinias.

Materials you will need:
sterile potting mix, a bucket, a sharp knife, rubbing alcohol, a narrow dibble, chopstick or pencil, a shallow flat with drainage holes, labels, and large plastic bags.

Prepare the nursery flat first by moistening the potting mix and pressing it into a clean flat. Now, using a knife that you've first sterilized in rubbing alcohol, neatly slice off a large leaf by its stem (take it from a large, healthy houseplant). Make a small hole, about half an inch (1cm) deep, in the waiting flat, and tuck the cutting into place, firming the mix around it. It's okay if the leaf now rests on the mix surface. Insert a label nearby so you remember the plant's identity.

Once the flat is full, cover it loosely with a plastic bag. Don't let the plastic sag onto the leaves or soil surface—if need be, elevate it with sticks at the corners or at intervals. Place the flat in a warm, sheltered spot, and check on it daily. Water it carefully if the mix begins to dry out, and ventilate it if too much moisture condenses on the inside of the bag.

After a month or two, you'll start to see tiny new leaves forming. When you are sure they're rooted, you may gingerly remove them and discard the large "parent" leaf you started with. Now you are ready to repot the baby plants.

Want to try out interesting propagation techniques? Having a potting table will give you the excuse you've always needed, and the motivation to do the projects carefully and neatly.

Storage Features

If you are purchasing a potting bench, you will notice a lot of variation in the storage options. Some benches are very elaborate and some are quite simple. A word to the wise: some features that look attractive may turn out to be hard to use (they are either too small, too far out of reach, or difficult to clean). Try to envision what your needs will be so you can make a practical decision.

SHELVES

The simplest benches have only one shelf, underneath, for handy storage of heavier supplies like containers of potting soil, larger tools such as watering cans, or stacks of occasionally used items such as flats and clay pots. If the shelf is slatted, you'll get aeration and maybe less warping or buckling over time but perhaps also occasional spillage onto the ground or floor. A lower shelf is also nice just to prop up a foot while working. The space under the lower shelf may also come in handy. If it's six or so inches (15 or so centimeters) above the ground, you can shove a few items under it, such as an occasionally used drying screen or your gardening clogs. If it's closer to a foot (30cm) off the ground, make use of the space by mounting coated-wire organizer bins under it.

Upper shelves, intended for smaller and lighter items, are practical only if they are within easy reach and out of the way of the main work surface. Since these shelves are obviously narrow, back and side rims are smart. Otherwise, they'd better be enclosed (like the back of a bookcase is) or backed by a wall or tall backsplash.

Two or more upper shelves are advisable only if they are neither flimsy nor too narrow. If you have a sturdy shelf system of two or more shelves, it's handy if the very top shelf just has braces front and back, so you can tuck in small, frequently needed items or display pots or small watering cans.

Add to an upper shelf's usefulness by putting pegs or hooks under it or along its front, for hanging gloves, trowels, and weeders. Another storage-expansion idea is to attach a caddy, either temporarily or permanently, for often-used tools like pruners and knives. Some potting benches come equipped with adjustable shelves that allow you to find the best placements of the shelves for all your needs.

DRAWERS, BINS, AND CUBBIES

Since you've decided to make the investment in a potting bench, the good news is that potting benches provide plenty of opportunity for consolidating the storage of tools and supplies. The bad news is that, in time, you may find it insufficient and begin piling or leaning additional items nearby. Perhaps this is not a big problem, if you've chosen a good spot. But be forewarned: for many gardeners, a potting bench is a stepping-stone to the longing for a full potting shed, with all the working and storage space you could wish for!

Some benches come equipped with one or two drawers just under the work surface. These are handy for stowing frequently used tools, sharp tools you want to keep out of sight, gloves, seed packets, and the like. However, exposure to the dampness that naturally comes with gardening projects may cause drawers to warp a bit, making them harder to open and close. To hold off this day, keep the drawer runners clean and (unless they are plastic) oiled.

Old drawers salvaged from a discarded desk or bureau make nice bins, best placed on the lower shelf. Other good choices for stowing soil and amendments or hand tools are strong plas-

tic tubs or small trash cans, large metal canisters, and wooden wine boxes. Lids are nice because they help keep out moisture and curious animals and may allow stacking, one atop another.

Cubbies are small storage receptacles intended for small things, like handfuls of plant tags, pens, pruning scissors, and so forth. Unlike those found in an old-fashioned secretary desk, potting bench cubbies should provide upright (not sideways) storage. Cubbies need not be bought from a store; many everyday gardening items, from small clay pots to mounted plastic sleeves, have been employed this way.

A salvaged dresser or desk is a super acquisition, if you have the space for it. Tuck useful items in the drawers and use the top for work, display, or additional storage.

Other Benches

For the resourceful gardener, there are certainly a number of alternatives to the traditional wooden potting bench. A little shopping around, or your own creativity, may provide you with one that is every bit as wonderful, and perhaps less expensive or more interesting.

METAL BENCHES

While you may have envisioned a wooden potting bench, metal ones are an interesting option. Some benches or potting tables are made entirely of metal, while others have a steel work surface and shelves but a wood frame. Metal has several distinct advantages. It is durable and easy to clean—just spray it off with the hose after each use. Also, such benches don't rot, and they resist rust. Galvanized steel, for example, makes for a very sturdy bench and provides a durable work surface. A zinc-coated surface will take a lot of abuse, and it is rustproof. Aluminum is lightweight and easy to clean, but it will show scratches; also, the supports on an aluminum bench should be made of a stronger material for support. Be sure you know the advantages and disadvantages of the material you want to use before you make your selection.

HOMEMADE AND SALVAGED POTTING BENCHES

Want to make your own? There's no reason why you couldn't. This way, you save money (though a cedar one will still prove expensive) and you will be able to customize. You can certainly borrow from the design of other potting benches you've seen or follow someone's plans (see the books listed in Further Reading),

A rustic shelf unit made of natural materials is a natural for a potting place, whether it houses supplies or displays plants, or both.

but if you decide to strike out on your own, here are a few ideas.

• Choose a table that's a good height for you and long enough; it should also be deeper than two feet (60cm). Set a bench (from a picnic table?) atop it and fasten this with nails or screws near the back of the table.

• Get an old door that has a window in its upper half. Support it on sawhorses, benches, chairs, or blocks—anything that raises it to a good height. Remove the glass and install a sink or plastic bin; alternatively, install some screen and place a bucket underneath.

• Salvage or convert an old boudoir vanity table. Complete the antique look by placing a washtub on its surface.

If space is limited, consider a smaller potting table, like this compact metal model. The high back-splash and elevated sides keep projects in bounds, plus there's a little storage space below.

POTTING PLACE PROJECT

Taking Hardwood Cuttings

This is a good autumn or winter project, because you must harvest cuttings from woody plants as they are going dormant. You will not be planting them until the following spring. Select vigorous, healthy-looking wood that grew in the past year; a general rule of thumb is to choose lighter-colored stems that are about the thickness of a pencil.

**Materials you will need:
sharp knife, damp towel, rooting powder, rubber bands, labels, and a box of damp sand.**

Out in the garden, cut several long stems. Wrap them in a damp towel. Take the bundle to your potting bench and shorten the cuttings to segments of about a foot (30cm) in length. Make a slanting cut on the top of each so you remember which end is up. Dip the other end in rooting hormone and tap off excess.

Bundle like kinds together using rubber bands and label them. Store them for the winter in a cool (but not freezing) place in a box of damp sand. You do not need to completely bury them. They'll form a callus on the bottom from which new roots will someday form; but you won't see roots form over the winter. The following spring, you may plant them in a prepared bed and nurture them until they do root.

Chapter Five

Life After Potting: Other Uses

Gardeners are natural recyclers—witness not only the compost pile, but also the salvaged items that get put to good use in the yard, such as an old step-ladder pressed into service as a stand for potted plants or the chopsticks relied upon as transplanting aids. The same resourcefulness can certainly be applied to your potting shed or bench when it is not in use or if you decide for some reason to take it out of service.

Outdoor Uses

The most beloved gardens become an extension of the home, particularly during the summer months. We eat meals outdoors, play and putter, and have guests over. Temporarily cleared of their gardening accoutrements, our potting places can be made useful or decorative, or both.

POTTING BENCH OR CADDY IDEAS

Thanks to its generally maneuverable size, a cleared-off potting bench can add wonderful ambiance to a summer gathering. Two strong people can deliver it to the best spot; if it's a caddy with wheels, positioning it or even shifting it from one location to another is so much the easier. If you are worried about guests or an errant pet or volleyball knocking anything over, be sure to place it away from the action a bit. If there is space, you may be able to temporarily stash the regular residents of the potting bench underneath it.

The most obvious practical use of your potting bench is as a buffet table. You can arrange utensils and napkins on the upper shelf, or place a large bowl of punch on the work surface, and line cups or glasses on the upper shelf. Or you can set out a few buckets of ice and soda pop or beer and have colorful plastic cups set next to the buckets for easily filling. If you are hosting a barbecue, the chef

If you like to entertain outdoors, an idle potting shed makes a good storage area for furniture as well as tablecloths, napkins, pillows, centerpieces, and so forth. Having everything so accessible means you can throw spontaneous parties on a moment's notice and keep your yard free of clutter the rest of the time.

OFF-SEASON DECORATIONS

There are scores of decorative uses for your potting bench year-round. Here are a few ideas just to get you started:

Autumn: Set your potting bench up on the front porch and display pumpkins, gourds, and sprigs of bittersweet. You can even place the bowl of Halloween candy here.

Winter: Place the potting bench in a sheltered location that is also visible from the street and adorn it with greenery, cotton batting (for snow), "Christmas village" houses and figurines, cute little birdhouses, hardy potted plants, or dried flower arrangements. Hang wreaths or swags on it. String lights along the upper shelf or around the entire thing. For a holiday party, a blooming amaryllis or two will forgive you if you set it outside on the table for a short time, and welcoming candles or a lantern could perch on an outdoor potting bench.

may appreciate having the table adjacent to the grill for the various implements as well as using it as a staging area for the food. Wheeled caddies have the added advantage of allowing you to easily haul the cooked burgers over to the picnic table (condiments, too), or make a grand entrance with a flaming baked Alaska in the gathering darkness.

Alternatively, the bench can serve a purely decorative purpose. Contributions from the garden arranged on the bench top are nice; consider loose sprays of herbs or

greenery, vases of flowers, or potted blooming plants. Or smother the entire thing in attractive arrangements. For an evening party, a potting bench is a lovely and relatively safe stage for a selection of candles or lanterns.

Of course, you know that your work surface will be easy to clean after the party is over—this knowledge can make your evening even more enjoyable.

CONVERTING A POTTING SHED

If it is possible to move aside, hide away, or otherwise store the contents of your potting shed, it can be put to other uses. Indulgent grandparents have been known to clear one out completely so the children can call it a playhouse and fill it with their toys for a while.

If you move and are unable to bring the potting shed along, prospective homebuyers who are not gardeners might want some ideas. The most obvious uses may be as a tool shed or storeroom. But tell them—or the real estate agent showing your property—that your little outbuilding can easily be made into a playhouse, requiring perhaps nothing more than a fresh coat of brightly colored paint. An artist may also wish to convert it into a studio—if the natural light is insufficient for a painter or sculptor's needs electrical lighting can be installed or upgraded. And if you have running water out there, and even a working sink, a potter or amateur photographer may be thrilled.

Opposite: An autumnal display of pumpkins and gourds is perfectly proper on an outdoor potting table. Right: If the potting shed is no longer required for gardening projects, it can be put to use as storage space. In addition to tools, the shed might also house bicycles, other sporting equipment, seasonal decorations, and so on.

PROTECT YOUR POTTING PLACE

If your potting bench, caddy, or island is outside year-round, you'll want to keep it covered when it is not in use so wind and weather don't damage it. Even indoor potting places need protection, not from the elements but from household traffic. Tossing a waterproof tarp or blanket over it usually provides adequate protection. If you want something more attractive or fitted, check out the coverings intended to protect lawn furniture, riding mowers, or barbecue grills—perhaps one of these will suit.

Indoor Uses

Some people take their potting bench or caddy out of service during the winter or acquire an extra one for practical household uses because they like the look and the convenient features. Thanks to its durable construction and easy-to-clean surface, it lends itself to many practical uses.

Mud room: If there's room in an entryway or breezeway passage, a potting bench becomes very handy. Boots and shoes can be piled on the lower shelf, and gloves, hats, and scarves can be tossed on the bench surface or tucked on a shelf or into a drawer, if any. Umbrellas can be leaned against it, and a bag or two of road salt can be stashed on the lower shelf. Lock de-icers, scrapers, and a flashlight can be lined up on an upper shelf where you can grab them quickly should you need them. All this keeps clutter to a minimum and out of the way of traffic.

PLAYHOUSE RULES

Sorry to say, conversion doesn't tend to work both ways; a child's playhouse is not easily made into a potting shed. Nothing about standard-issue playhouses is adult scale. For starters, there's the height—you'll forever be bumping your head. And there is the low, narrow door and small windows that don't provide adequate lighting. Lastly, many children's playhouses are made of heavy-duty plastic, unsuitable for installing hooks, shelves, or anything else nailed down. Wooden ones are often rather flimsy (constructed of cheap plywood), again unsuitable for the needs of a busy, tool-laden gardener. The only exception is a deluxe playhouse made by an accomplished carpenter for older children; if you are lucky to inherit such a building, it may convert to your needs, with some modifications.

Hutch: If your bench is not too rustic or can be painted or decorated to go with a room's decor, invite it into the house proper. Keep large, attractive bowls on the work surface, display china plates against the backsplash, and line up your delicate teacup collection high above harm's way on the upper shelf or shelves. Or use it for displaying and storing placemats, napkins, tablecloths, coasters, and the like.

Pantry: Tucked into a small room or closet, or into a corner of the dining room or even the cellar, a bench can be very useful for storage of canned goods and other non-perishable items like pasta and baking supplies. To make storage more attractive, you could put some items in large canisters, bowls, or wicker baskets. Hang aprons from a hook to one side.

Bar: Especially when you are hosting a party, but even when you're not, a potting bench or caddy on wheels serves as an ideal bar. Bottles of liquor or wine can be set on an upper shelf, and buckets of ice, glasses, napkins, and coasters can be arrayed on the work surface. Extra supplies can be stowed on the lower shelf. For a slightly more elegant personality, adorn it with fine glasses, a port and brandy collection, a cigar humidor, ashtrays, and a bowl of matchbooks.

Dining room buffet: For an informal meal, a potting bench is an ideal place for appetizers, bags and bowls of snack foods, utensils, plates, and napkins. Or perch some hot plates, a crock pot of hot soup, or a coffee maker on its surface. For a big holiday meal, keep the roast or turkey here, along with the carving knife–out the reach of little hands but still nearby in case anyone wants seconds.

Foyer stand: A potting bench or caddy can make a handsome yet practical feature of your home's entryway. You and your guests can leave your keys, purse, backpack, gloves, hat, or sunglasses here while inside. The shelves can be decorated with flower arrangements, greenery, knickknacks, or candles. Road maps or canvas bags for shopping can be stashed on a shelf or in a drawer.

Bathroom table: Imagine how pretty a smaller bench might be when stationed in your bathroom or a guest bathroom. Toiletries and soaps can be displayed on the surface, and towels, washcloths, and spare linens can find a home underneath. Add a few candles, figurines, or a vase of flowers fresh from the garden.

Sewing or other craft project table: The surface is perhaps too high for a sewing machine (unless you bring over a stool to sit on), but any project that requires that you spread out can be accomplished here. Supplies and tools such as scissors and glue can be shoved towards the back, if it's deep enough, or perched on an upper shelf.

When the flurry of spring and summer gardening activities are over, find more uses for your potting place. Its cool, tidy interior might be ideal for curing and storing harvested fruits, vegetables, flowers, and herbs.

OFF-SEASON USES FOR A POTTING SHED

There's no need to take everything out of the shed when winter comes, but if it's uninsulated or you simply don't plan to return for any substantial projects until spring, you can certainly take advantage of its shelter in other ways.

....
- Hide holiday gifts
- Stash Christmas tree before and after use
- Store barbecue grill
- Store bicycles
- Pre-chill bulbs
- Store seasoned firewood
- Confine an unruly pet while animal-wary guests are visiting

---

Sources

The following companies offer various tools and supplies, including potting benches and caddies.

Allen, Sterling & Lothrop
191 U.S. Route 1
Falmouth, ME 04105
207-78104143

Alsto's Handy Helpers
P.O. Box 1267
Galesburg, IL 61402
1-800-447-5785

Berry Hill Limited
75 Burwell Road
St. Thomas, Ontario
Canada, N5P 3R5
1-800-668-3072

Cart Warehouse
P.O. Box 3
Point Arena, CA 95468
1-800-655-9100

Catamount Cart
P.O. Box 365
Shelburne Falls, MA 01370
1-800-444-0056

Charley's Greenhouse Supply Co.
1599 Memorial Highway
Mount Vernon, VA 98273
1-800-322-4704

Dan's Garden Shop
5821 Woodwinds Circle
Frederick, MD 21701
301-695-5966

Gardeners Eden
P.O. Box 7307
San Francisco, CA 94120
1-800-822-9600

Gardener's Supply Co.
128 Intervale Road
Burlington, VT 05401
1-800-863-1700

Homestead Carts
2396 Perkins Street N.E.
Salem, OR 97303
1-800-825-1925

Jackson & Perkins
S. Pacific Highway
Medford, OR 97501
1-800-292-4769

Kinsman Company
River Road, P.O. Box 357
Point Pleasant, PA 18950-0357
1-800-733-4146

Langenbach Tools
644 Enterprise Avenue
Galesburg, IL 61401
1-800-362-1991

Lee Valley Tools Ltd.
P.O. Box 6295, Station J
Ottawa, Ontario, Canada K2A 1T4
1-800-267-8767

Lehman's
P.O. Box 41
Kidron, OH 44636
216-857-5757

A.M. Leonard Company
P.O. Box 816
Piqua, OH 45356
1-800-543-8955

Mellinger's
2310 West South Range Road
North Lima, OH 44452
1-800-321-7444

Moose Growers Supply
P.O. Box 520
Waterville, ME 04903
207-873-7333

Niwa Tools
1333 San Pablo Avenue
Berkeley, CA 94702
1-800-443-5512

Ozark Handle and Hardware
P.O. Box 390
Main Street
Eureka Springs, AR 72632
501-253-6888

Peaceful Valley Farm & Garden Supply
P.O. Box 2209
Grass Valley, CA 95945
916-272-4769

Plow & Hearth
P.O. Box 5000
Madison, VA 22722
1-800-627-1712

Smith & Hawken
117 E. Strawberry Drive
Mill Valley, CA 94941
1-800-776-3336

The following companies offer potting sheds, potting shed kits, or potting shed plans:

Dalton Pavilions, Inc.
20 Commerce Drive
Telford, PA 18969
215-721-1492

Gardensheds
651 Millcross Road
Lancaster, PA 17601
717-397-5430

Heritage Garden Houses
311 Seymour Street
Lansing, MI 48933
517-372-3385

Smith & Hawken
117 E. Strawberry Drive
Mill Valley, CA 94941
1-800-776-3336

Summerwood Products
190 Konrad Crescent
Markham, ON L3R 8T9
Canada
1-800-663-5042

Valley Oak Tool Co.
448 West Second Avenue
Chico, CA 95926
916-342-6188

Further Reading

The following is just a sampling of books in which do-it-yourselfers will find construction plans and ideas for potting sheds and potting benches.

Ortho Books. *Garden Construction*. San Ramon, CA: Ortho Books, 1985

Stiles, David and Jeanie Stiles. *Garden Projects You Can Build*. Shelburne, VT: Chapters Publishing Ltd., 1995.

Swift, Penny and Janek Szymanowski. *Build Your Own Outdoor Structures in Wood*. New York: New Holland Publishers, Ltd., distributed by Sterling Publishing Co., 1997.

Index

Photo Credits

©Derek Fell: 16 left

The Garden Picture Library: ©Lynne Brotchie: 12; ©Linda Burgess: 38, 72, 123; ©Georgia Glynn-Smith: 71; ©John Glover: 34, 74, 76; ©Sunniva Harte: 22, 66; ©Jacqui Hurst: 15, 29, 78 right, 105; ©Ann Kelley: 70; ©Mayer/Le Scanff: 10-11, 87, 94; ©John Miller: 28; ©Nick Meers: 60-61; ©Stephen Robson: 35; ©Ron Sutherland: 46; ©Juliette Wade: 13, 43 right; ©Mel Watson: 95

Courtesy Garden Sheds, Lancaster, PA: 51, 54, 81

©Michael Garland: 16-17; 92-93 (designed by Joseph Ruggiero); 98 (designed by Nancy Powers); 113

©Giammarino & Dworkin: 14, 68-69, 88, 91

©John Glover: 8, 26 right, 53, 63 right, 99, 120

©Annie Gordon: 61 right, 102 left

©Jesse Walker Associates: 104, 114

©Lynn Karlin: 24-25, 27, 41, 43 left, 44-45, 55, 75, 78 left, 79, 83, 102 right, 103, 118-119

Courtesy Langenbach: 26 left, 107, 109, 115

Midwestock: ©Jeff Morgan: 73

New England Stock Photo: ©Rixon Photography: 82; ©Michael Olenick: 50; ©Kevin Shields: 4-5, 116

©Clive Nichols: 47 (designed by Jonathan Baillie); 63 left, 117

©Hugh Palmer: 2, 6-7, 9, 18-19, 20, 23, 30-31, 33, 40, 42, 45 right, 52, 56, 62, 65, 77, 80 both, 84, 85, 86, 97, 108, 110, 111, 121

©Betsy Pinover: 112

Positive Images: ©Mikki Ansin: 58-59; ©Patricia J. Bruno: 89; ©Karen Bussolini: 48-49, 59 right, 90 left, 96, 100; ©Jerry Howard: 19 right, 32, 57, 64

©Eric Roth: 36, 37

Courtesy Smith & Hawken: 90 right, 106

Courtesy Suncast: 101

Tony Stone Images: ©Linda Burgess: 21; ©Myron: 39